David Skopec

Digital Layout

for the Internet
and other Media

	Layout, the Design	Layout, the System	Layout, the Experience
Scope			
Base area			
Action			

Layout – three perspectives

Digital media is a multifaceted and constantly developing area. Whether at the level of planning, conception, usability design or programming, each stage requires an understanding of some fundamental concepts, and each can be assessed and discussed in some detail.
This book focuses on questions related to design and so contributes to the decoding of this complex topic. As a component in observing digital media it centres on exciting and informative aspects, which help in understanding fundamental interconnections – while at the same time opening our eyes to the possibilities.

The structure of this book follows three perspectives on layout: the design, the system and the experience. These perspectives are not arranged according to the process, but rather are devoted to the different areas under discussion. You could even say they correspond to the designers' view of the layout; that of the development team and the users.
Design, system and experience form three pillars, divided horizontally here in the contents into three sections. These are then interlaced with three levels of approach: scope, base area and action. From whichever angle you observe the subject of layout, there is always a logical connection – the holistic view.

Content

	Layout, the Design	Layout, the System	Layout, the Experience
Scope			
Base area			
Action			

Layout and interface

If a book talks about "layout for digital media", we should clarify what we are dealing with here. After all, the term "layout" is juxtaposed in the jargon of media design with "interface". Often they are both used to mean the same thing, although upon closer inspection they express different things.

"Interface is not a thing," Gui Bonsiepe writes in his book "Interface – Design neu begreifen", "but the dimension in which the interaction between body, tools (hard- as well as software) and behavioural aim are structured."[>0.1-1]

This extremely precise description opens up a clearly delimited scope of definition for the layout: layout as a reflection of the interplay between communicative, cultural and cognitive aims, as the visual manifestation of the interface.

And this type of distinction is useful, since unfortunately the users often see themselves confronted with simple, undifferentiated "screen design". This is why the aim in media design should be to consciously bring about the synthesis of both dimensions – "layout" and "interface" – instead of assuming a diffuse mixture.

In this book the term "layout" primarily describes the formal and semantic aspects of a digital application, while "interface" means the function and interaction.

This may not exactly clarify the terminology, but in this context it allows us to outline a viewpoint that focuses on the layout from a design perspective. Seen in this way, a connectable model of media design is produced, which allows for a consistent linking to a number of technical, editorial or ergonomic aspects – and also demands this.

Scope of Ideas

Where to begin? Concentrate on what? How to create the space for ideas? Design works best with a good concept. As far as the development of conceptual ideas is concerned, we must eliminate the idea of the ingenious inspiration. A well-structured approach and calculated breaking of the rules are often of greater help.

Scope of Action

What does the virtual material feel like? Are there sharp edges in the digital world? What happens to the layouts beyond the visible range? The digital scope of action is composed of numerous dimensions, that influence the design – in this way a definition of the format, structuring and grid systems facilitates the planning and realisation.

Scope of Effect

Despite all the much-praised flexibility offered by digital media, it is irrelevant as to what scope of effect a layout is developed for. Some may be clearly differentiated and equipped with a profile of relevant demands for the layout – the prerequisite for a truly adequate use of digital media.

Elements and Objects

The layout controls the interplay between all the visual components in the interface – and these may vary in their purpose and appearance. An initial overview of the central components and their characteristics leads to orientation and allows priorities to be made.

Ordering and Structure

As far as the comprehensibility of a digital system is concerned, ordering and structure play an extremely important role. They help users recognise the characteristics of an interface, without the need for many explanations. And they form the basis for a standardised layout of the contents and a systematic project development.

Perception for the Layout

Questions about human perception are interwoven throughout the design process. These fundamentals are summarised in one chapter, so that a clever linking of cognitive aspects does not result in an impenetrable tangle. The important basics of cognitive processes are laid out without the formal-aesthetic ballast.

Montage

Montage turns several individual parts into one functioning whole – not only in the technical sense, but also in its semantic dimension. The arrangement of figures, base area and time becomes in itself a powerful design tool, as long as it is used consciously. The result is a visual gesture: the dynamic overall expression in connection with the individual visual elements.

Collaboration

A layout is not only the finished result of work – it is also a tool in itself. It becomes an essential basis for work and communication whenever a project needs to be realised or further developed. This demands instruments that can communicate a layout in a clear, meaningful way.

My Layout

Anyone can design. And with some digital applications this is made particularly easy. However, the obligation of explicit design leaves off where it becomes a personal concern of the user – everyone with their own contents and with a corresponding layout. Design without a layout: the examination of the possibilities alone sheds new light on the basics of popular ideas about design – and provokes further thought.

Layout as a process

Along the route from the idea to the completed digital application, work on the layout passes through many stages of action. From the brief to the final evaluation there is hardly any one completely self-contained design phase. And, with the exception of the one-man show, a team of specialists is usually involved in the development of a digital application, all of whom add their particular views on the layout. For some this ends with the visionary prototype, for others it begins with the dimensions down to the last pixel for technical reasons. Working on the layout is a process that cannot be limited to visual questions, but is systematically linked to all aspects of the digital medium – often under completely new assumptions.

Systematic or systemic?

If we observe the different stages of a digital project, it seems as if there is a chronological sequence, suggesting a linear, systematic way of operating. But this is an optical illusion: in reality the various stages demand a high degree of flexibility.

What about changing the structure on the day of the deadline? Developing elements in the style guide before the actual detailed concept? Producing rough designs while simultaneously evaluating the prototypes? Why not? The dynamics and possibilities in working with and for digital media have highlighted the fact that instead of a systematic adherence to rules, a systemic understanding is becoming increasingly important; ways of working that penetrate the subject matter as a whole and grow with it.

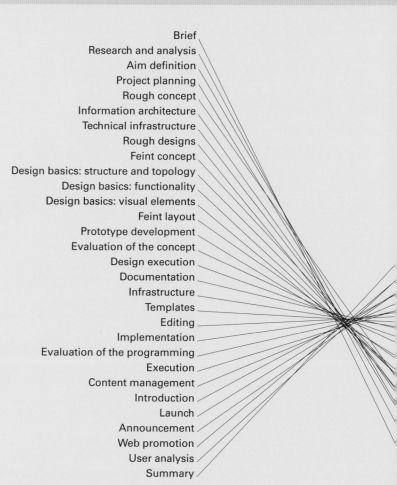

Brief
Research and analysis
Aim definition
Project planning
Rough concept
Information architecture
Technical infrastructure
Rough designs
Feint concept
Design basics: structure and topology
Design basics: functionality
Design basics: visual elements
Feint layout
Prototype development
Evaluation of the concept
Design execution
Documentation
Infrastructure
Templates
Editing
Implementation
Evaluation of the programming
Execution
Content management
Introduction
Launch
Announcement
Web promotion
User analysis
Summary

A good example of this is the separation of form and content. As opposed to traditional media, in the field of online media in particular a layout concept may be commissioned before the exact contents are finally agreed[>2.2]. In addition, interactivity and user-guided interests can have a direct influence on the layout's appearance[>3.3]. In this way, shapes occur, which no one has ever designed before, filled with contents, which are only compiled at the moment where they are first accessed. The classic interplay between form and content takes a back seat – while the design of possibilities comes to the fore. And this represents the challenge, since the design of possibilities far exceeds trying out technical variations. The aim is to keep an eye on the qualities of true communication – one that reaches the user and helps providers to convey their message.

This is only possible when the designer becomes part of the entire development process, understands it and helps shape it – assuming an integral comprehension of the layout as a process.

Documentation, analysis and archiving of project progress and results

Evaluation of server statistics and direct user feedback, optimisation

Add to search engines and Web directories

Cross-media communication on the launch of project

Going online, distribution of the media

Training in the editing system and maintenance

Administrative and technical establishment of the (editing) system

Upload to the server or production of the media

Test under normal operating conditions, debugging

Programming of all the pages necessary and the technical components

Preparation of the contents necessary such as text, photos or audiovisual materials

Creation of templates for an efficient realisation of the project

Preparing the technical infrastructure: hosting, databases, editing systems

Drawing up of a style guide for the realisation of the project

Design of all necessary page types

Testing the technical and design functionality, comparison with given aims

Technical realisation of the design using a functioning prototype

Design of prototypical pages

Definition of the visual elements: picture concepts, colour environments, graphical components

Development of navigational and functional elements

Determining page types, development of design grid and coding

Condensing the possibilities into one visual concept

Approaches: development of design possibilities

Evaluation of the technical requirements

Development of a detailed contextual and technical structure

Overview of contents: setting priorities and rough structure

Definition of scope, schedule and costs

Development of project aims and strategies

Target groups, competitors and media surroundings

Client's requirements and aims

1.1.0

Recognition

Where to begin? Any approach to a task presents the
designer with the same challenge: what is the first step?
Design, without question, is more than just a "superficial"
– in the most literal sense of the word – occupation. And
even if you make the most concerted effort to approach
the design of a layout in this way, you will soon be
corrected by the somewhat more complex reality –
especially where digital media are concerned.
The task has been worded, the brief is completed, but have
all the questions been answered? And this is a question
that only each individual can answer. This is why a project
can very easily be approached with a "wanting to know".
And in most cases you will see that several questions

Impulse questions

24 questions that could be the start of "wanting to
know". Certainly incomplete, yet so fundamental
in their nature as to cover a broad spectrum of
questions. None of these questions has a single
answer – indeed they lead to further questions that
help to create as complete a picture as possible of
the task in hand. Or by consciously ignoring them
they provide the necessary scope.

remain to be clarified before you can even start to look for appropriate solutions. And to get it over and done with straight away, many answers only become clear during the work process, while others will hopefully remain unanswered. Because there is nothing more boring than a concept that has an answer for everything.

Yet "recognition" goes far beyond answering questions. It means becoming aware of the problem areas; becoming clear about the tasks and realising the potential possibilities. But this only works when the questions lead to probing: curiosity, with a little welcome discomfort, coupled with the motivation to improve. This is because probing is a central task in designing: identifying the aims, questioning their meaning and definition, countering supposedly ultimate guidelines with a healthy dose of

scepticism and investigating their true value. In designing for digital media this applies in particular to the areas where elite interface and usability gurus announce their functional definitions of the new media, in order to dispense with the need for a conceptual and design-orientated discussion by labelling it "artistic toying around".

"Recognition" is an important part of the design process and leads to independence and superiority. And it is only this that allows for an autonomous stance with regard to communicative and formal criteria.

Questions to be answered during the design process

Specifications that should result from the planning and listing of tasks

Aim
How is the idea behind the project and its scope defined?

Audience
Who is it aimed at?

Contents
What type of contents and how are they made available?

Guidelines
What are the communicative, formal and structural specifications?

Technology
Are there technical demands and responsibilities?

Benefits
What benefits can the user and provider expect?

Time frame
How much time is available?

Budget
What financial means are available?

Media suitability
Which medium offers the best potential?

Significance
What impression is to be conveyed?

Mental model
What allows an associative orientation?

Character
Is the design orientated towards familiar means of expression?

Form
What do the designs look like?

Structure
How are the designs structured in terms of contents and function?

Functionality
How does the interface work?

Taxonomies
How are the components named and ordered?

Definitions to be agreed upon depending on the social, cultural and economic context

Innovation
What is novel?

Originality
What makes it special?

Relevance
What creates personal associations?

Novelty
What makes it contemporary?

Conventions
Which rules apply and are useful?

Habits
Which habits could be useful, and which not?

Meaning
What makes it recognisable and identifiable?

Value
What values are conveyed?

Possibilities

Digital media basically allow for the dynamic and multi-dimensional presentation of contents and structures within a system. There is not just one way of making contents available, but several ways in most cases. There is not simply one way to structure a system, but many ways available. And there is not just one way to use a system, but numerous. In many respects, digital media are open and variable, making them "implicit" media. Traditional media on the other hand are "explicit", that is to say fixed in their materials and layout at the time of their creation. And this is an important difference in terms of concept and design. The concept phase with digital layouts firstly begins with a collection of possibilities, which allow variable, implicit approaches to the solution. Here, "possibilities" is really meant as comprehensively as it sounds: it includes aims, contents, structures, technologies and much more, which directly, indirectly or sometimes at first sight have nothing to do with the project.

To gain an overview at this stage it can often be useful to extend the virtual workspace of the computer to include the real space of the working environment. This makes the entire collection of possibilities more present and visible, instead of compacting them to fit the format of the computer screen.

Collecting and filtering is an important part of the concept phase. As such, it is initially very abstract – and at the same time very dynamic: collect, order, dissolve and reorder. Here the idea is to make the unclear clear, to select the suitable possibilities from the myriad on offer and to follow up their core ideas consistently. Filtering, in this case, means a clever reduction of complexity and is in no way a unique, final process. Whether systematic or playful, the demands made on the design of a layout may repeatedly be seen in the light of changing possibilities and so lead to various approaches to a solution.

Ideas

Ideas need working on – especially in design. And contrary to popular opinion, sudden, ingenious inspiration is seldom to be found. That which is spontaneous and original is usually the result of an imaginative, yet simultaneously, systematic approach. Developing a good idea takes time and room to think. Extensive analyses and refined strategies may form an important basis for this in visual communication – and should indeed be used as a platform. Even from an academic point of view, the design should always be along pre-defined lines; the design idea has often enough considerably influenced the communicative direction. Thus the area of inspiration in design can and should be approached much more openly

Idea: process and stimulus

Organisation theory in economic or computer science differentiates between two types of problem definitions: "ill-structured" and "well-structured". Both may be applied one-to-one to visual design:

"Ill-structured" problems
These are mainly based on unknown variables, with no known solution methods. This corresponds to design tasks that require a new solution. Thus the variables first need to be clarified and different solution methods tried.

"Well-structured" problems
For example, a mathematical task, where the variables and calculation methods are known. This is similar to a design task that has to be solved according to strict specifications, such as those in a design manual.
Such tasks are best solved by routine.

Many design tasks contain both "ill-structured" and "well-structured" problems and so require both routine as well as creative efforts. The proportions should be identified as the first step, since routine allows rapid progress, while creative work presupposes a corresponding amount of time to experiment.

than may be assumed from the contents of the design brief. Seen in this light, an idea – even in design – is always the synthesis of various possibilities. Or, as Hermann Hesse put it: "In order to make something possible arise, the impossible has do be tried again and again." However, today there is still no theory of how to design and even Albert Einstein, to add another opinion, had to realise that there is no logical route to innovation. Yet there are at least pointers to that which almost certainly hinders inspiration. Often a task provokes an impulsive action to find a solution. This reflex action is usually contained in internalised terrain and entails a direct evaluation as a premature censure. But inspiration and evaluation should occur independently of each other. Whoever is over convinced of the sudden quality of a spontaneous approach will hardly make an effort to look for alternatives. Yet whoever is interested in researching broader areas should consciously overcome this spontaneous reflex and retain an openness for further events. And initially the quantity of the ideas is clearly more important than their quality. Their evaluation takes place in a second stage.

Visual communication presupposes an openness for change. This is not only a philosophical question, but also a fundamental demand on human perception [> 3.2]. This is namely orientated above all towards perceivable differences. Thus, good ideas in design do not necessarily have to be sensational innovations – it is often simply those that count on a conscious breaking of the rules.

There are numerous "creativity techniques" for developing ideas – and even more opinions as to what use they are. Less spectacular, but certainly very useful, is a basic classification of the methods for developing an idea or executing the design operations, as developed by Werner Gaede in his book "Vom Wort zum Bild" [>1.1-1]:

Systematic approach
This is based on the systematic collection and modification of components, characteristics and means of expression: such as by structuring and restructuring, enlarging and reducing, combining and extracting, replacing, adding, mirroring or reproducing.

Stimulated approach
This is a conscious or subconscious search for inspiration from an external repertoire: in the surroundings, media, in discussion, libraries, etc. The main concern here is the development of analogies and associative approaches, which are then further developed into individual solutions.

Intuitive approach
This is the development of a thought process, which is primarily based on internalised perceptions and knowledge, that is to say an internal repertoire. This type of thought process may occur spontaneously, without being evoked specially. This is actually a systematic process that takes place subconsciously.

Preventing the "scissors in the head"
Finding ideas and the evaluation of the results should be clearly separated – which is not always easy. Nevertheless, this type of reflex action may be overcome in stages by:

… sketching the direct route of execution and thus identifying the reflex action.

… sketching as many additional approaches as possible, simple and complex, logical and absurd, close and distanced. There is hardly ever just the one.

… compiling the approaches and ordering them in terms of different and, where possible, contrary viewpoints.

… identifying the core principles and bundling similarities to form compact approaches.

Rhetoric

Freed from the process of inspiration a conceptual framework of ideas can greatly enhance the development of the design process; a basic orientation that serves convincing and effective communication. These days, principles of rhetoric act as helpful guidelines for this type of orientation, although we are more familiar with them as techniques for speaking and writing. The term "visual rhetoric" is derived from verbal rhetoric, and this established form may be excellently applied to visual conception, as well as to other media-communicative fields. Even if at first it sounds like it, visual rhetoric is in no way just an academic domain, but provides a superb aid for determining and expressing the characteristics of a

Logos

Subject matter forms the basis for logos within the rhetorical triangle. Above all, the concern here is the practical solution of how to convey function and content by way of design. This includes such factors as legibility, comprehension and availability. Logos stimulates intellectual perception by way of expert competence and an intelligent thought process in the visual preparation. Logos may derive from the preparation of the contents, yet usually occurs in digital media due to factors such as user navigation, layout structure and arrangement of the given information.

design, such as the layout. The basis for this are the three forms of persuasion: logos, the rational appeal; pathos, the emotional; and ethos, the moral appeal. The ancient Greeks knew that rhetoric discourse is determined by the intentional balancing of these three forms of persuasion; they are concerned directly with the thoughts, feelings and convictions of the target audience.

The counterpart to this balance of the three forms of persuasion is emphasis on one of the three appeals, which occurs often and usually unintentionally. For example, an emotional emphasis (pathos), whereby a media scenario is mainly directed at the feelings or a rational emphasis (logos), which underscores the factual information. What is interesting with digital media is that their mainly technical character (logos) leads to the emotional (pathos) and moral (ethos) means of persuasion moving to the background – which quickly results in a certain inapproachability in a digital application. Yet because pathos and ethos in particular are responsible for affecting perception as well, it is no doubt helpful to pay particular attention to these. Usability, normally only discussed, for example, on the logos level, thus becomes a rhetoric, holistic matter, which all three forms of persuasion definitely need to include. Using the model of visual rhetoric it becomes clear that digital media are not concerned with technical-cognitive aspects alone, but also with the impression and values they convey.

Ethos

The disposition of an appearance is conveyed using ethos. Its concern is with values and moral aspects, such as trustworthiness or durability. The appearance of a digital application may be articulated in different ways: does it appear traditional, modern or avant-garde? Ethos is the subtle way of steering an expression, which the target audience primarily interprets using existing value patterns. Digital media are often accused of having an innovative yet unstable disposition, not least due to their continuous technical advances. Therefore, a design requires a special effort in order to reflect the values of trustworthiness and durability.

Pathos

Whether something appeals to us emotionally mainly depends on pathos in the design preparation. Pathos stimulates our feelings and subconscious means of perception. This covers the whole range of design elements: choice of form and colour, visual elements, symbols or materials. In many ways digital media can live out their technical characteristics particularly well here, such as when it comes to the integration of time-based and auditory means of expression, when interaction emphasises the users' interests or when the contents are aligned with a particular target audience by way of personalisation. > 3.3.3

Design

A "design" is not only merely the result, but also the very process of design. Design usually takes place iteratively, that is to say in a gradual, repetitive approach. The path to the finished result is determined not least by making things visible: notes, structural diagrams, models, sketches, scribbles – every method of visualising thoughts and ideas, contributes to the success of the design. The same applies to everything that aids an exchange of thoughts and ideas – a discursive design process – since the development of an analogue, as well as a digital medium, often presupposes collaboration between several specialists. Concept creators, copywriters, designers, programmers, to name but a few, continuously participate in the development and need to input their contributions in a communicable form. And with digital media in particular, with their potential often situated at the edge of the conceivable, a continual visualisation of contents and structures, of spatial, temporal and interactive dimensions, is a crucial aid to the communication. And optimal communication in the exchange of thoughts is more important during the development process than the brilliance of the individual, as communications specialists repeatedly emphasise. Many designers – specialists in making things visible – play a very significant role here and take on a particularly high degree of responsibility.

Making things visible during the design process should be consciously distinguished from the forms of design realisation and be of a noncommittal, experimental type. Demonstration and modelling away from the monitor is of critical importance here: initiating a media break and thus freeing the unfinished and imperfect from the pressure of realisation. This creates space for criticism and optimisation, lowers the threshold for questioning and actually allows for experimentation. Designing and trashing are the two complementary poles in the design process, which mutually determine each other and can only lead to a convincing solution by way of a reciprocal relationship.

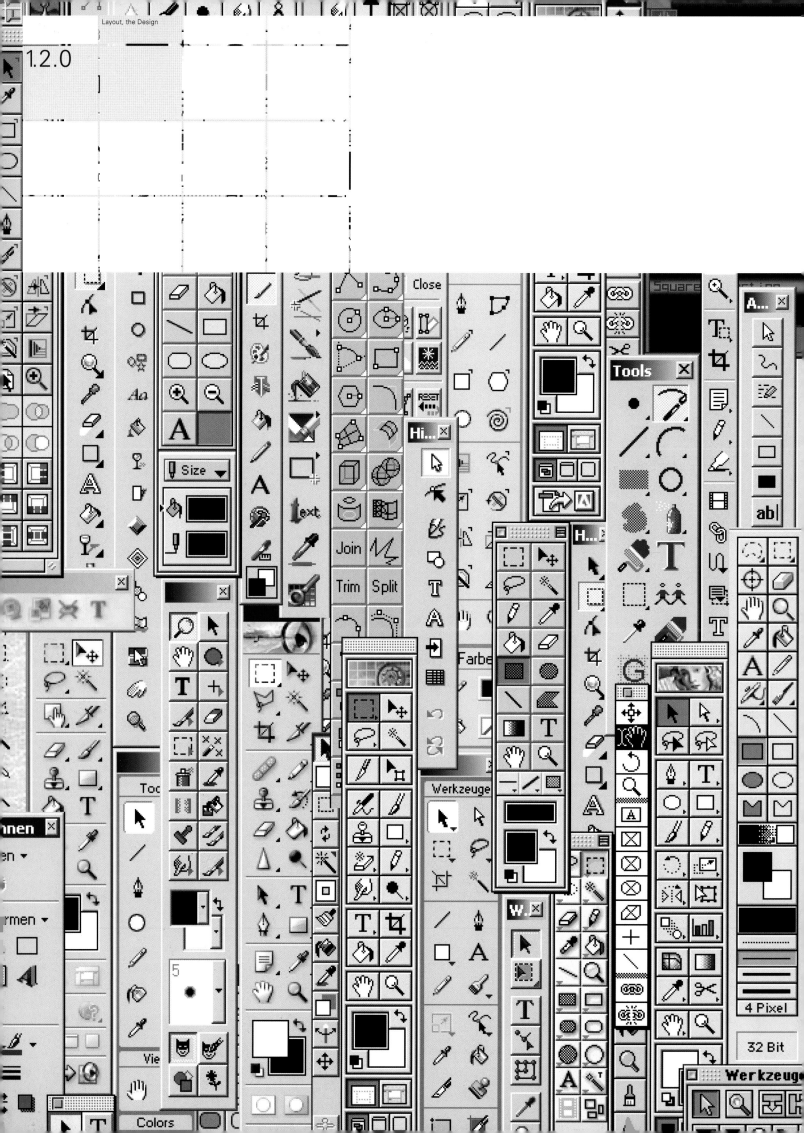

1.2.0

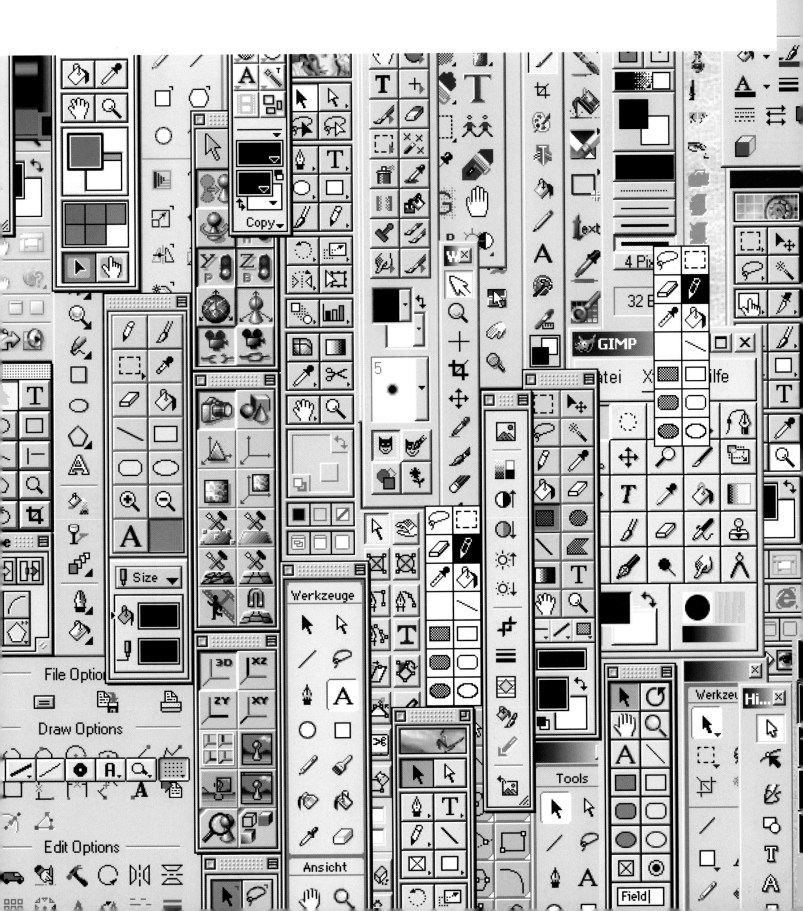

Layout, the Design

1.2.1
Elements and
Objects

Elements of the dynamic
layout

Elements of the dynamic layout

A layout is composed of a number of different elements, such as typography, dots, lines and shapes, each of which is very basic in nature. It is only by carefully selecting, combining and determining such characteristics as their shape, size and position that these elements lend the layout its own appearance, while a repetition of such characteristics conveys the character and aim of a digital application. But what are the characteristics of the typography, what part do graphical elements play, how are picture elements used and – of considerable importance – how is the system of navigation and navigational elements conveyed?

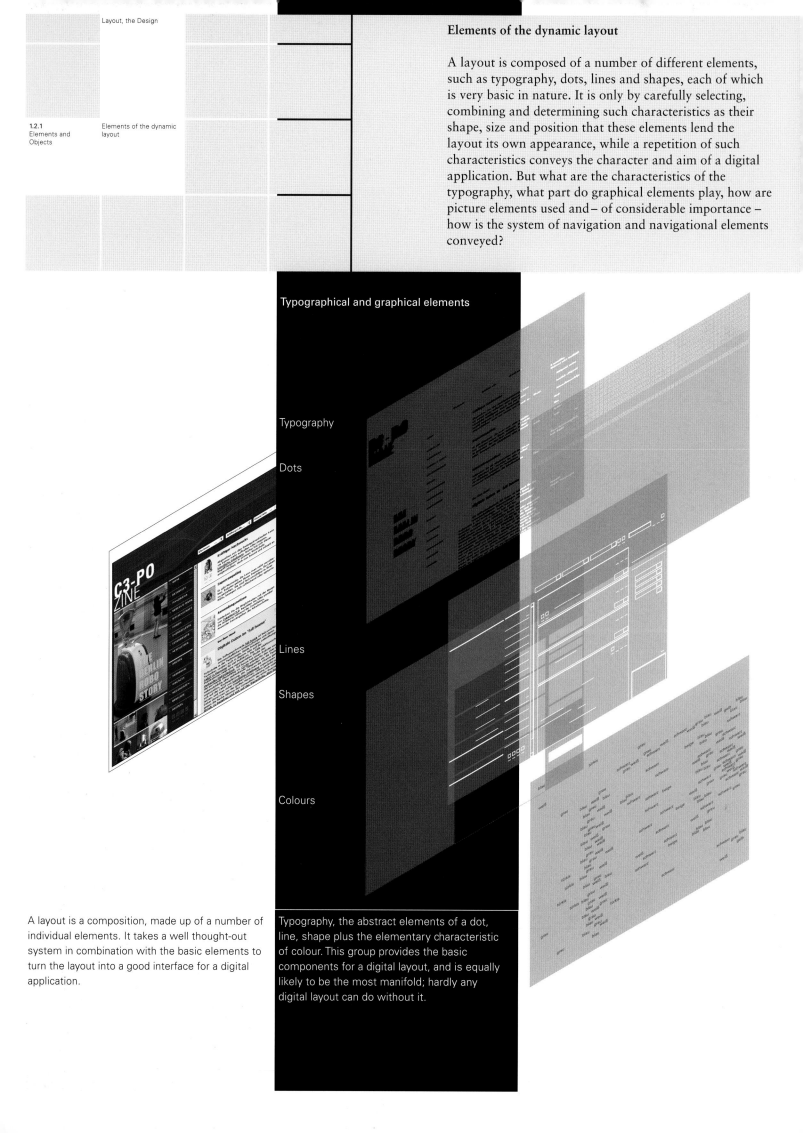

Typographical and graphical elements

Typography

Dots

Lines

Shapes

Colours

A layout is a composition, made up of a number of individual elements. It takes a well thought-out system in combination with the basic elements to turn the layout into a good interface for a digital application.

Typography, the abstract elements of a dot, line, shape plus the elementary characteristic of colour. This group provides the basic components for a digital layout, and is equally likely to be the most manifold; hardly any digital layout can do without it.

Ideally, the answer to these questions may be found in one continuous system, which can be consistently applied to the layout of a digital medium, in turn contributing to the user-friendliness of that medium.

The levels of a fictitious website shown here demonstrate how they would look split up into their individual components, assuming they could be extracted so easily; because, in reality, most layout elements are closely interrelated in terms of their characteristics. Here, the first group is formed by the basic graphical and typographical elements: typeface, dots, lines and shapes. Assigned to these, on a second level, are the colour characteristics in an abstract form. The second group is composed of picture elements such as photography, illustrations, symbols and icons. And finally comes the third group, formed by the functional elements of a website.

Not all of the elements shown here are necessarily part of a layout, yet they often play a significant part – in very varying degrees of importance. Text receives a coloured background, buttons are differentiated by a combination of symbols or dots joined as textures to form shapes – to name but a few examples of the combination and interaction among basic elements. Many of these may be freely designed, while others are based on standards that may be taken from the range of functions within an operating system: the toolbox. Buttons, scroll bars or pull-down menus are typical examples of available tools, and are often found as components of a layout.

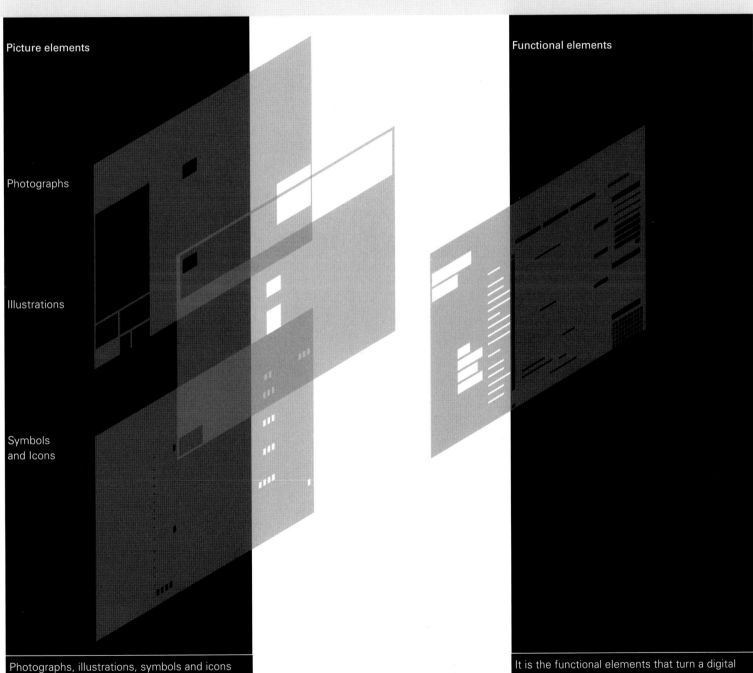

Picture elements

Photographs

Illustrations

Symbols and Icons

Functional elements

Photographs, illustrations, symbols and icons are the eye-catchers within any layout. The picture contents and their language are a promise of direct information, which can be easily and quickly absorbed. They should be used carefully due to their very popularity.

It is the functional elements that turn a digital layout into the interface for a digital medium. It is here that individuality is separated from the mainstream: either original designs or taken from the standard range found in the operating system's toolbox. And this is where it gets exciting, because we often have to first develop the functions for ourselves that we would like to see in an innovative system.

Typographical typology

Providing a layout is not entirely composed of HTML text – the typographical elements within a digital layout may be divided into two groups: first of all, the group with typographical elements serving the organisation of the interface, such as page headings, navigational elements, labels, etc. The other group is used in the typography to convey the contents. While both groups may primarily transport text information, they are treated differently in terms of design. User-friendliness is certainly one important reason for unmistakable, visual differentiation of the two typographical groups.

Organisation typography:
Page header
Everything that could point to the type of document and the communicator – and at the same time a recurring part of a layout. Often connected to graphical elements and is also often used as such.

Organisation typography:
Navigational elements
Basic component of a digital layout. Should be viewable regardless of the software and hardware used – and is also used for labelling in connection with graphical elements.

Content typography:
Body and headlines

And a consistency within the layout spanning several types of document is no doubt the other important reason. Because while "content typography" should remain as adaptable as possible, the "organisation typography" of a layout tends to be more static, so as to reliably fulfil its purpose regardless of the type of document, application software or even the hardware. This is why the "organisation typography" is consistently treated more like a fixed element, while the "content typography" is usually treated as dynamic, flexible and adaptable text.

cineastas

FIND LOVE IN 7 D

, de bajo costo, resulta mas facil poner
r Jason Silverman.

TIME BONUS SECTION/GLOBAL BUSINESS/PHARMACEUTICALS

Jungle Medicine

Natives want a share of the profits when drug firms exploit their remedies

17:00	RE 33609	**Rostock Hbf**
		Rostock Hbf 14:07 - Güstrow 14:34 - Waren(Mü 16:47
		täglich , nicht 24. Nov
17:00	RE 33609	**Rostock Hbf**
		Rostock Hbf 14:13 - Plaaz 14:39 - Waren(Müritz 24. Nov
17:00	S S7	**Potsdam Hauptbahnhof**
		Potsdam Hauptbahnhof 16:30 - Potsdam-Babe Savignyplatz 16:59
		30. Okt bis 14. Dez 2002; nicht 2., 3. Nov
17:00	S S75	**Berlin-Wartenberg**
		Berlin-Wartenberg 16:46 - Berlin-Hohenschönhau

Specialty Sites

Categories

Global Sites

DRUCKVERSION ▸▸
ARTIKEL VERSENDEN ▸▸
LESERBRIEF SCHREIBEN ▸▸

MORE ON THIS STORY

Recent**Articles**

Business | Techno

new topic   post

■ Nation

Log In | Register

Deutsch | Français

Print this article   Send to a fr

Smart Search

FIND
GO

Ideally, all forms of content typography should remain in an editable text format, which means in most cases TrueType fonts in ASCII format. This allows for easy changes to the content and helps in organising the amounts of data to be transferred. Here, hyperlinks take on the role of hypertypography; they aid navigation and yet, at the same time, are content.

Organisation typography:
Labelling and functions
The sole purpose of a large number of typographical elements is to serve the structure and functional expansion of a digital layout. These, too, are usually used in connection with graphical elements, such as shapes, lines or symbols.

The typology of reading

Hypertext undoubtedly represents a prototype for the "non-linear reading" of text; links between different text units allow information to be contextually processed. From a typographical viewpoint, the networking of different users has also brought about new ways of working with typography, optimised in terms of interaction and dialogue, as may be seen in the well-known examples of newsgroups and Web-based forums. Yet our typographical layout forms have been established in the same way, corresponding to classical media in their number of typographical applications. Reading types, as described, for example, by Hans Peter Willberg and Friedrich Forssman in their book "Lesetypographie" [1.2-1]

Links:
- Think Secret: Neue iMacs?
- Apple: Neue Power Macs

▶ Thread-Übersicht

- **Apple aktualisiert angeblich morgen die iMac-Linie** - ms am 03.02.2003 um 09:28 Uhr

  - **Ich wünsch mir ich wünsch mir ich wünsch mir ...** - swiss-ives am 03.02.2003 um 09:39 Uhr

  - **Na, was fehlt denn da noch?** - MacMat am 03.02.2003 um 09:44 Uhr

    - **iBooks mit BT und Airport-Extreme!** - Udo am 03.02.2003 um 10:57 Uhr

    - **Wer weiß** - DrWatson am 03.02.2003 um 10:59 Uhr

      - **Re: Wer weiß** - Zadian am 03.02.2003 um 11:37 Uhr

        - **Re: Wer weiß** - moehnetiger am 03.02.2003 um 15:4

    - **Schnelle, günstige MACs mit aktueller Technik! n/t** - Drakon am

      - **Ketzer!!! ;-) n/t** - MarkInTosh am 03.02.2003 um 12:28 U

        - **Jehova, Jehova! :-) n/t** - truth am 03.02.2003 um 14:

    - **100.000 Songs auf 40 GB ? Wow...** - EveryMac am 03.02.2003 u

  - **Re: Apple aktualisiert angeblich morgen die iMac-Linie** - Windtaenzer

▶ Bitte loggen Sie sich ein, um einen neuen Beitrag zu schreiben.

Conversation on the Internet

Linear reading
(e.g. articles)

HARPER'S MAGAZINE

WEEKLY REVIEW

NOVEMBER 12, 2002

Defying historical trends, the Democratic Party managed to lose control of the Senate during a midterm election Richard Gephardt responded to his party's catastrophic failure by announcing that he will not seek reelection as House minority leader, he will instead prepare for a presidential run in 2004. France and Russia, after weeks of dickering, voted in favor of a United Nations Security Council resolution on Iraq after the United States agreed to change the word "and" to "or" and the word "secure" to "restore." "This would be the 17th time that we expect Saddam to disarm," said President George W. Bush. "This time we mean it. This time it's for real." American officials claimed that the resolution was a "mousetrap" that gives the U.S. the right to go to war unilaterally, Europeans pointed to assurances from American diplomats that the document contains "no hidden triggers." President Bush settled on a war plan for Iraq that will include a short air campaign followed by rapid ground operations involving about 250,000 troops. Administration officials confided that they were hoping for a defiant challenge from Saddam Hussein rather than a slow drawn-out refusal that could fritter away the strategically important winter months, which are the best time for fighting a war in the Middle East. "I think a lot of people are saying, you know, gosh, we hope we don't have war," President Bush said. "I feel the same way." A million people converged on Florence, Italy, to protest the coming war. French prostitutes took to the streets in Paris to protest new restrictions on the sex trade. Communists in Russia marched to protest the betrayal of

---

www.macnews.de
The Internet as a medium of dialogue between several users has led to applications for typography very similar to those of verbal conversation. At the same time, many digital layouts are based on typographical structures that we know from classical media. The examples shown here are mainly composed of typographical elements.

www.harpers.org
Linear reading – considered by many as unsuitable for use in digital media as too difficult – has still secured its own place in online magazines for example.

for the classical media, are used in many forms of digital layout as well; often even in a technically extended way, aiding efficacy in the editing and perception.

The reading types here, on the other hand, show defined standards for typographical design, such as are found, for example, in the field of learning or cognitive sciences to distinguish between different reading types. Considering this typology of reading for digital layouts is founded in the interdisciplinary process of change within the media, such that the traditional media are strongly influenced by digital media, which in turn are based on numerous fundamentals of traditional media, it makes sense to extend this typology by aspects of perception on the screen. >3.2

Consultative reading
(e.g. search engines)

Selective reading
(e.g. portals)

Differentiating reading
(e.g. tutorial)

www.google.com
With this type of reading a particular piece of information is sought, such as in a dictionary or manual. Key words and definitions are highlighted to facilitate the search for specific terms.

www.aldaily.com
The reader gains a rough overview, browses through the text and filters out the relevant information. One typical text read in this way is the daily newspaper and corresponds, for example, with the portal of an online magazine.

www.selfhtml.teamone.com
The most careful type of reading is applied to those texts, from which we want to learn as much as possible, such as textbooks. In the world of digital media this type of reading is often used for tutorials and training programmes.

Dots

Strictly speaking, the dot is a square and the smallest graphical element within a digital layout – and, technically speaking, corresponds to a pixel on the screen. Everything else shown on the screen is composed of this tiniest unit. Yet the dot also has its own design application – in an abstract form, for example, in creating textures, in a depictive form in an illustration, or as a structural form in creating the layout. Its square shape greatly influences the design of a layout, and in this way at least has contributed to its own "pixel aesthetics", as is found in many different forms in the field of screen design.

Due to low screen resolutions, early examples of computer graphics, such as the "Galaxions" game, required their own, optimised presentation. Despite ever-increasing monitor resolutions, this has developed over the years into a visual form of expression in itself, characterised by the pixel.

www.k10k.net
The layout of this website is mainly based on textures composed of dots. Here, a uniform texture is used, which differs simply in terms of the colour spectrum and shading depending on the application.

Diffusion and dithering of individual dots generates the impression of shading.

Individual dots arranged in a regular matrix produce a shaped texture...

With the ever-increasing improvements to monitor resolutions and the more widespread use of vector-based imaging technologies, the "visual square" of the pixel is losing its significance. At the same time, there is more freedom to use a dot again in an undefined graphical shape as a design element. However, for the time being, this requires an optical compensation of basic square shapes; interpolation using intermediary shades.

The smallest dot in the display is a pixel. It is only by interpolation using intermediary shades that it appears round.

www.nylon.media.mit.edu
The simple frequency and positioning of individual dots creates the impression of a spatial context.

www.sodaplay.com
Here, individual dots form the coordinates for an object, which can then be animated using different settings...

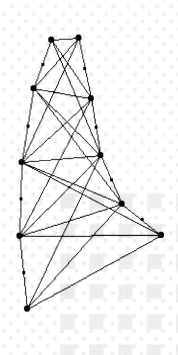

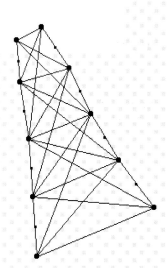

...whose characteristic appearance is strengthened by grouping or by recurring distances.

Dots may be used in their square form as illustrative and stylistic characteristics.

When used as coordinates dots take on a structural or even visualising form; a spatial one in this example.

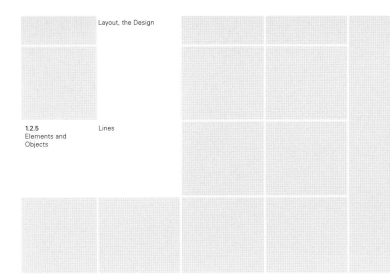

Lines

As one of the important basic graphical elements, lines are used in an abstract, structural or visualising way. Abstract, when they are used, for example, in rows to form textures. Structural, when lines separate or highlight different areas and information within a layout. And visualising, when they are used in illustrative or explanatory figures.

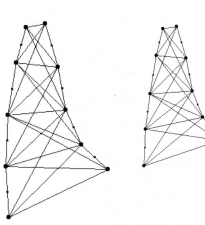

...yet it is only by linking the coordinates with lines that the tower takes on its typical image.

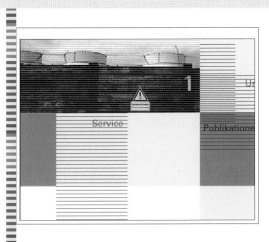

www.asstech.com
On this website textures made of lines mark the different rubrics, which allow a view of the selectable rubrics as the mouse passes over them.

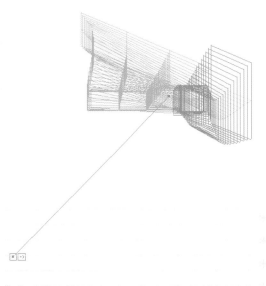

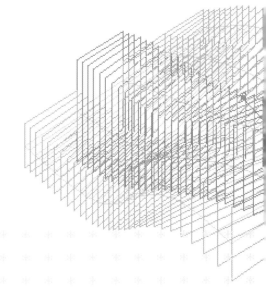

Regular textures made of lines of varying thickness can create a spatial impression.

A line is composed on the screen by a row of pixels, whose thickness is defined in pixels, and thus may be hard to recognise with high resolutions and small thicknesses. Conversely, with low resolutions a line may easily be mistaken for a shape. Similarly, the use of diagonal lines is not a problem with high resolutions, while the stair-stepping effect becomes visible with lower resolutions, which then has to be compensated for using interpolation. In terms of design, working with lines in digital layout allows fine, simple, but rather technical-looking images. A reduced layout may be composed of text, images and structural lines, and would be effortlessly understood as an interface for a digital application.

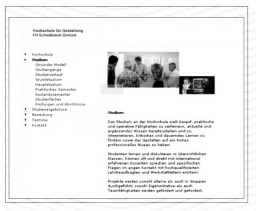

www.hfg-gmuend.de
A system of lines structures the layout of this website by way of header, navigation and contents. The reduced use of lines conveys a clear, neutral image and may be flexibly modified.

www.unipublic.unizh.ch
On the University of Zurich website a texture of lines is used to mark the site and to illustrate typographical elements.

www.irrationalcontraption.net
This is mainly made up of a navigational environment that is controlled interactively and three-dimensionally. The whole visualisation takes place in frames, represented by different coloured lines. The overlapping frames create a spatial, technical impression.

The order and structure of a layout may be created by a division using lines.

By shortening and the use of perspective, a few lines suffice in order to create a spatial context.

Lines are suitable for reduced, neutral visualisations and create a technical, constructed image.

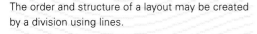

Shapes

The use of shapes in a digital layout is mainly focused on linking and less often on visualising or even illustrating. The use of rectangular shapes in particular may easily be realised on the orthogonally arranged pixel matrix of a display, and is thus correspondingly often part of a digital layout. Diagonal, round, oval or even amorphous shapes normally demand more programming work and visualisation techniques, and thus are better suited to vector-based environments (e. g. Flash).

Regardless of the technical aspects, the digital world seems to be rectangular, since almost every interface requires an unmistakable structuring of the layout area into its various components. Solving this by using rectangular shapes is an

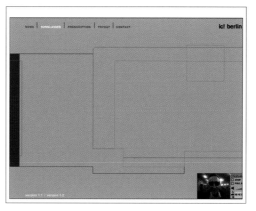

www.ic-berlin.de
Shapes as the dominant design elements form the basic structure of the interface and are in a continual process of change throughout the entire application.

www.onemedia.com
This online shop has positioned the rectangle as a central image; no doubt useful, considering the possible modular combinations among the range of products on offer.

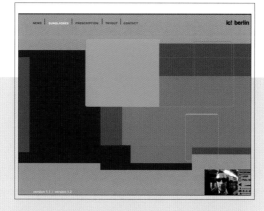

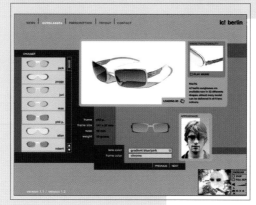

Within a digital layout shapes mainly take on a structural function.

obvious method, also when considering the perception aspect, since we are used to absorbing lots of information line-by-line and row-by-row >3.2 – as a glance at the layout elements in this book shows.

At the same time, the use of rectangular shapes as structural elements within the interface allows a simple, modular structure for a digital application. >2.2

Shapes are, apart from their structural potential, very gratifying design elements, as they automatically cover part of the layout area and may be simply filled with colours and textures. Yet all in all, the use of shapes leads to a "tectonic", static-looking use of the basic graphical elements – surely a good reason to try something different.

www.wz-berlin.de
Shapes, again as structures, but this time also visualising – because here the arrangement of rectangular, diagonal and round segments suggests the post-modern architecture of this Berlin institute.

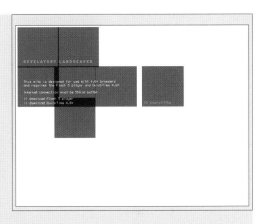

www.sfmoma.com
To mark an architecture exhibition, San Francisco's Museum of Modern Art's website featured an animated arrangement of shapes to visualise the architecture on display, with a permanent basic pattern.

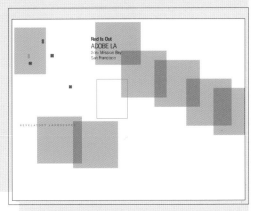

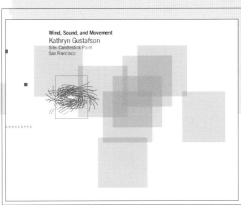

Used in large numbers, shapes can decidedly dominate featured a layout.

In irregular, possibly even dynamic form, shapes can even take on an illustrative role.

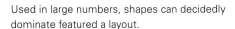

Colour

Colour, as an important characteristic of a graphical and typographic element, is a central components of a digital layout. Because of its ability to classify and convey meaning we know colour from all fields of our visible world. In our perception, colours are never neutral: they always evoke an association for us.

Aside from the many aspects of colour perception >3.2 the observations made here should firstly concentrate on the use of colour in digital layouts. And this is different to that of traditional media due to one major factor: colour is always available and more or less for free. While print production is still always concerned with the number of colours involved in a piece of design work, the digital

Colour as a signal

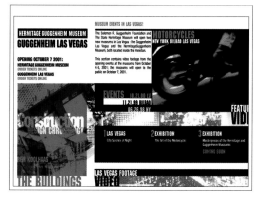

www.guggenheim.com
The Guggenheim in Las Vegas with a corresponding layout in black and red. A targeted and careful use of colour may be very effective and full of impact.

Light, bright colours attract our attention. This effect is specifically used wherever visual amplitude is concerned.

www.izumi.co.jp
The choice of colours shows that this department store obviously has a lot to offer. The digital shop window acts just like the one in the real world.

world can make use of the entire spectrum. And where the aim is to attract the user's attention, for example, the general rule applies: the more, the merrier. This is in contrast to the accentuated use of colour, which is supposed to be well thought-out, but can at least be as effective. Nowhere else are the well-kept clichés among traditional colour symbolism as obvious as on the Internet. For example, the entire blue spectrum of the international business world is spread out only a few mouse clicks apart. And nowhere else can the most yearned-for colour combinations be so easily fulfilled than on the Internet: a whole virtual world just in pink.

Colour has different meanings in different cultural circles. More about this in the chapter dealing with "Perception" >3.2.

Europe:	Nature
Arabia:	Islam
Japan:	Technology
USA:	Traditional

Colour as a symbol

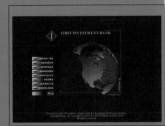

www.bankofscotland.co.uk www.bankgesellschaft.de www.tibank.bg
www.colmencapital.com www.jpmorgan.com www.allianz.com
www.bcl.ln www.chase.com www.closept.com
www.ml.com www.munichre.com www.tylor-companies.com

Blue as the colour of seriousness – many banks and other financial services appear to trust the symbolic significance of blue.

www.barbie.com
Pretty in pink – a whole virtual world revolving around the Barbie doll.

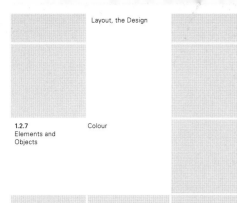

1.2.7   Colour
Elements and
Objects

Apart from its uses for attention-grabbing and symbolism, there are also completely sober, neutral applications for colour. For example, where labelling or ordering is concerned, colour becomes an indispensable part of the digital layout. Yet it is here in particular that care is needed; because the distinction of colours is limited by a human being's perception >3.2 – and equally by the reliability of colour imaging on the screens of the global Internet community. >3.1

And, finally, we know the more familiar area where colour as a means of visualising makes use of our everyday experience of colours; when dealing with spatial impressions or moods, for example – colour as a means of stimulation.

Colour to order

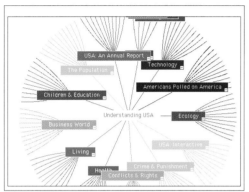

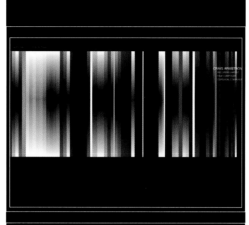

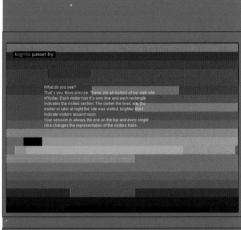

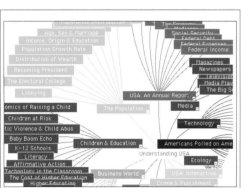

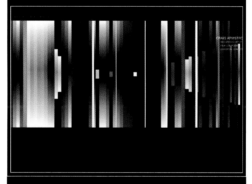

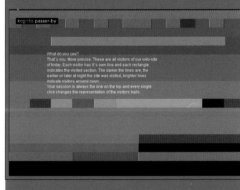

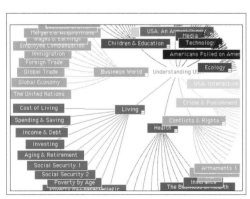

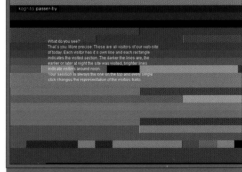

www.inxight.com
In this application the colours are used to label the individual areas of a website. Yet the choice of colour is too different or similar, making relationships and differences difficult to recognise.

www.craigarmstrong.com
The bars on this site stand for different tones that can be heard by passing the mouse over them. The greyscales are used to visualise the frequencies.

www.kognito.de
Here the visitor statistics on the website is visualised, each horizontal bar represents a visitor and the different coloured sections stand for the different rubrics. The brightness of the colours is linked to the time of the visit; the darker it is, the later or earlier in the day.

Colour to visualise

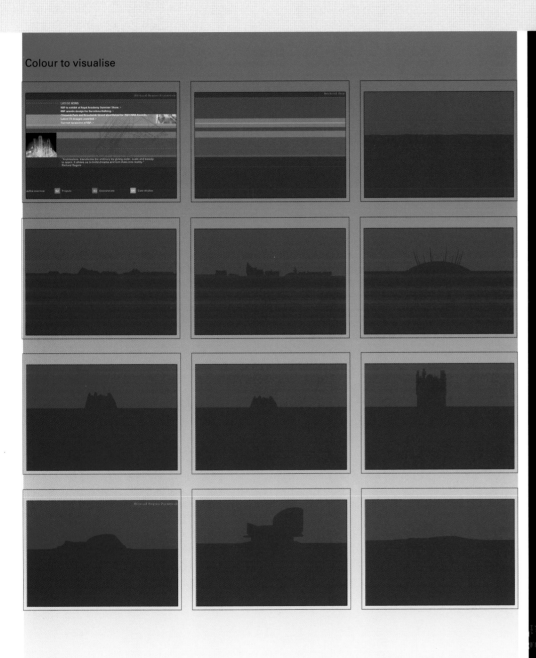

www.richardrogers.co.uk

The architect Richard Rogers visualises on
his website the silhouettes of the buildings he
has designed – and makes good use of our
experience of perception, so that we see colours
on the horizon as various shades.

Visual Who

This project by Judith S. Donath visualises a
group of people, where those who are less
closely linked to the group are shown in
darkened shades. Like in real life, where
the light source in the foreground becomes
weaker towards the background, and things
appear darker.

Photography

New equipment and technology have also greatly facilitated the use of photographs in digital media. Scanners, digital cameras and numerous processing options have led to photography becoming the ever-available design element, such that the uses of photography have become wider. Manipulation of a digital image is now an integral part of a digital layout – and this has resulted in the most varied forms of visualising photography. Positive, negative, blurred, lightened, discoloured – the range of possibilities is huge.

Black and white

www.barkowleibinger.com
Unusual in the colourful world of the Internet, a photographic concept in black and white.

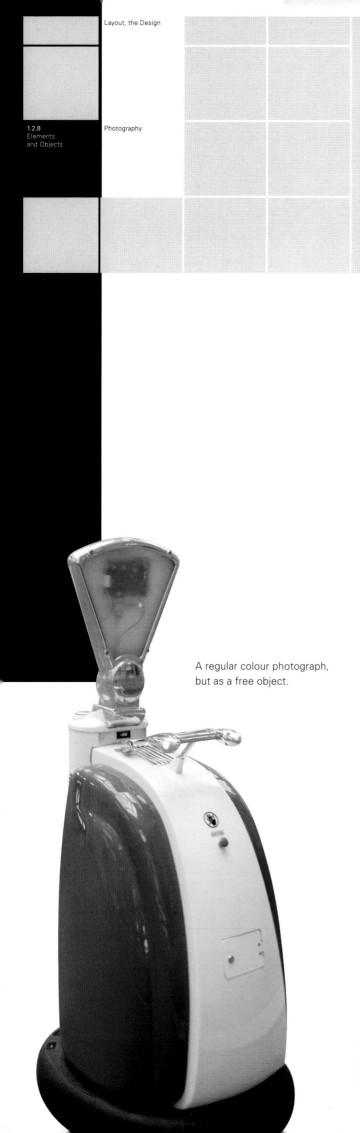

A regular colour photograph, but as a free object.

Blurry

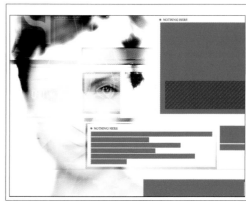

www.overage4design.com
A mainly blurred portrait, heavily reworked and only partially recognisable as a photograph.

And the greater the freedom, the more sense it makes to define one unmistakable visual language of photography within the layout concept. Is it to be used for visualisation or is it more illustrative? Does it retain its contextual function, or does it serve the identification, that is to say the graphical organisation of the interface?

Duplex

www.zavesmith.com
Photographs in black plus one additional colour.

Brightened

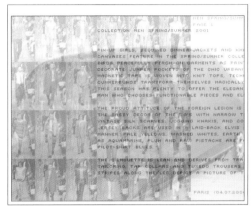

www.kostasmurkudis.de
All the colours in the photograph have been lightened with white so as to reduce their profile.

Strong contrast

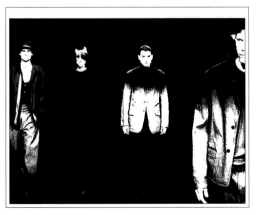

www.isseymiyake.com
All the colour values of the original were divided into black or white depending on their brightness.

Negative

www.integral.ruedi-baur.com
Short picture sequences in which the colours have been inverted.

Among the various applications for photography in digital layouts, that which is concentrated on an illustrative quality has become almost a rarity. Large picture formats and file sizes are without doubt more difficult to integrate within a digital application – and this is what makes them something special. Photographs that tell a story, show something in a simple way or set the mood for a certain topic add value to each means of communication and turn it into an experience for the user.

Storytelling
1:0 Brazil vs. Germany, final of the football world cup. Photographs can tell wonderful stories – but require a generous and corresponding treatment within the layout.

The use of this type of photography requires a clear concept, which needs to be agreed upon with the photographer prior to the work on the layout. The layout idea, with its visual language focused on photography, demands a restrained use of the remaining layout elements, since the contents of each picture are influenced by their surroundings.

Presenting
www.artemide.com
The Italian lamp manufacturer Artemide has something to show; even with small images, the photographic concept shows the effect of each lamp. And despite the number and diversity of images the photographs all remain within one harmonious colour range, without appearing monotone.

www.topshop.co.uk
If you want to sell on the Web, then you have to ensure your products are presented clearly and attractively.
The photographic quality of these clothes is designed for optimum recognisability. The lighting was chosen so that even online the characteristics of the material can be deduced.
The presentation of the products has been harmonised so that they can best be compared with one another – and customers can make the right choice.

Mood-setting
www.huskycz.cz
The Czech outdoor clothing manufacturer Husky uses atmospheric landscape images on its website, which invite us to go hiking – coupled with generous portraits of men and women alluding to the special relationship between man and nature. Of course the products are also shown, but as the very linking element.

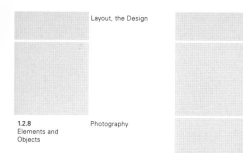

If the photography refers to a number of visualisation forms, then this should be in connection with the aim of the application. This is because a photograph can take on another function other than that of illustration; for example, that of labelling, when coding rubrics. Here it is less important what the photographs show, but rather how well they may be differentiated. This similarly applies to a contextualised design of the layout; decisive here is a thematic approximation and the visual impression, preventing the layout becoming too full of empty space – where this is not desired. And, as a graphical element, photography also takes on a function beyond that of pure illustration in the organisation of an interface, e.g. as a button, loading status or structural shape.

www.mpib-berlin.mpg.de
The "virtual tour" of the Max Planck Institute for Human Development is mainly based on photographs.
These take on not just an illustrative, but also a labelling and coding function. Depending on the context, they label the rubrics, become status bars or shape the surroundings.

Different details from photographs form the labels for the various rubrics...

... the selected detail stays put and becomes the loading status for the Flash application...

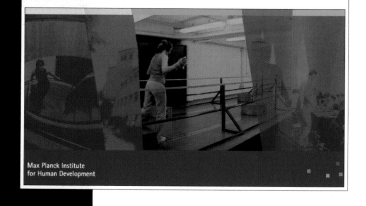

Whether as a label for rubrics, loading status, an illustrative image or a contextualised background, the type of photograph and the selection of detail need to match the purpose.

...the photo takes on its illustrative function in connection with typographical elements and...

...finally becomes the contextualised background for further windows.

Illustration and animations

The use of illustrations in digital layouts is so varied
that it cannot be orientated towards any pre-defined
methodology. There are, however, certain types of
illustrative figures that take on a special role when applied
in particular to digital media. These include the group
of photorealistic illustrations found precisely at the point
where photography reaches its limits. These illustrations
allow unusual perspectives and certainly add to the
fascination radiating from the world of digital images.

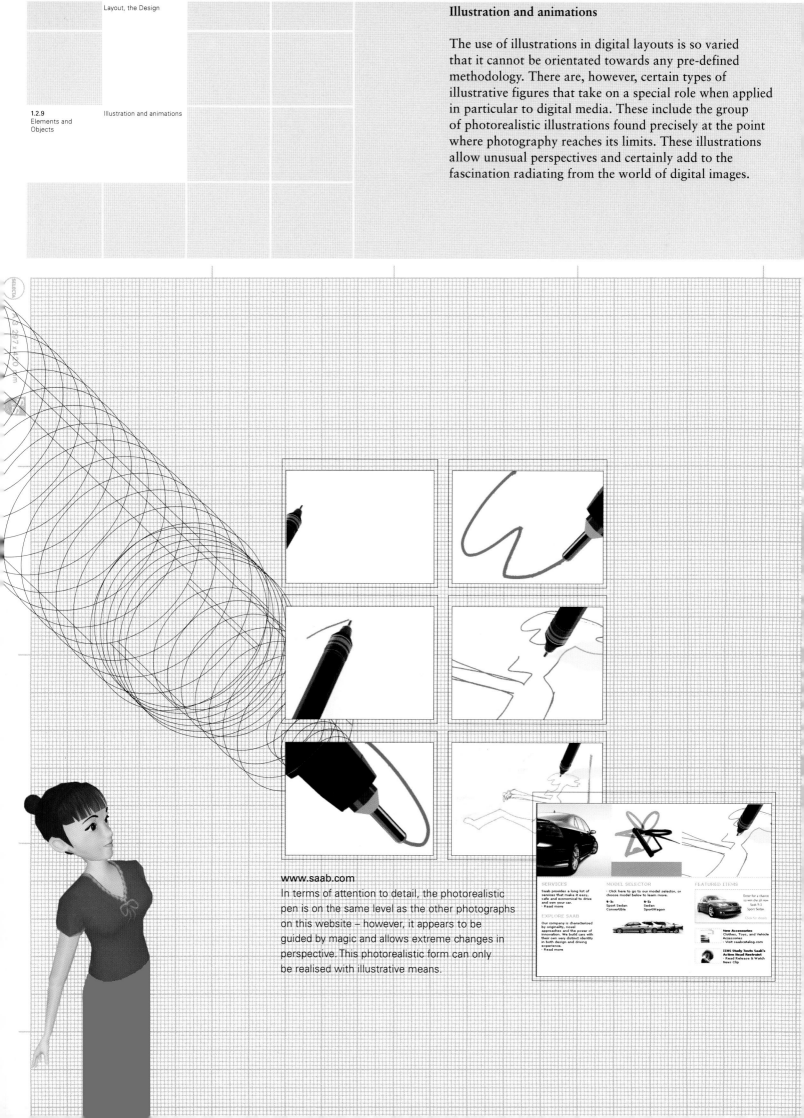

www.saab.com
In terms of attention to detail, the photorealistic
pen is on the same level as the other photographs
on this website – however, it appears to be
guided by magic and allows extreme changes in
perspective. This photorealistic form can only
be realised with illustrative means.

Illustrations are used in another area, since they can idealise an image and may be programmed such that their order and behaviour can be controlled. This allows them to be equipped with interactive features, as is the case with artificial figures, technical models or scientific explanations, for example.

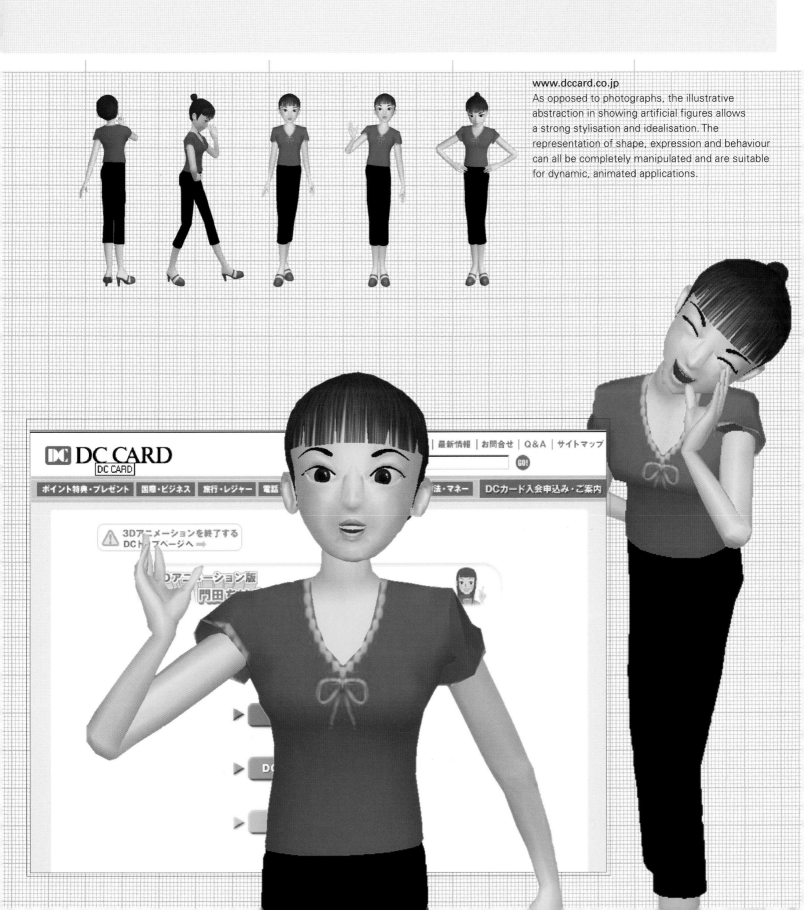

www.dccard.co.jp
As opposed to photographs, the illustrative abstraction in showing artificial figures allows a strong stylisation and idealisation. The representation of shape, expression and behaviour can all be completely manipulated and are suitable for dynamic, animated applications.

Illustrations may be based on completely different forms
of expression; from an artistic brushstroke looking like
an ink drawing, or a drawing created by hand, right up to
high-tech 3D models that could theoretically fly.
When using illustration in digital layouts, a stylistic
uniformity contributes to the consistency and thus to the
effect of the image. This is achieved, for example, by a
simple choice of colour scheme, defining line thicknesses
or even by the specific use of certain tools.

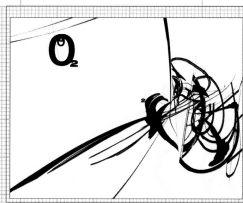

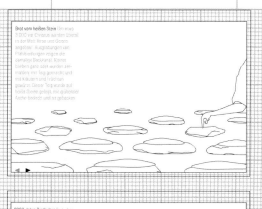

www.cmart.design.ru
The ink drawing on the screen in an artistic
illustration – an obvious hint at the strong
illustrative character of this website.

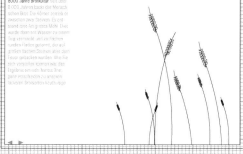

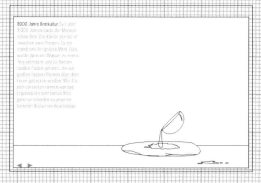

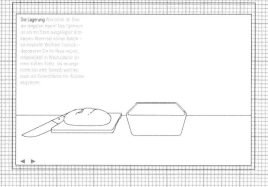

www.bulthaup.de
The history of bread making illustrated using
animated drawings, which become narrative
elements. The neutral implementation is
concentrated on the content level.

200 mal Brot Das lockere, weiche
Brot, so wie wir es lieben, gibt es
erst seit etwa 150 Jahren. Hepräsentativ auf die Auswahl zwischen
rund 200 verschiedenen Brotsorten und 1200 Arten von Kleingebäck.

Brotkultur im Mittelalter Großer
herausbildete sich in Deutschland
Klöster das Backen und um im
Mittelalter entwickelte sich das
Beckerhandwerk zu einem strengen
Zunft vor harten Regeln und
Strafen. Miniaturen aus dem
wurde "abschmecken" und der
Umschlang eines Backofens
trotz vielfältiger deutlichen
Bestimmungen. Die Bäcker aus
Mittelalters brachten es oft zu
sagenhaftem Reichtum.

Auch Hefebrote ein Genuss
Hefebrote, ob weiß oder grau, aus
man dagegen noch. Auch hier
gibt es große Unterschiede.
Die entlohnen wichtig kompliziert
von Aroma und Teigstruktur ist
das Resultat von fertigen Backmischungen und Maschinenbacken.
Wohltrat kann sehr käuflich dem
Auch hier der Tipp, sich nach
einem Bäcker umzusehen, der die
Schnellbackmethode nicht praktiziert. Auf alle Fälle zu vermeiden
sind fertig geschnittene Brote.
Sie sind fast feuchtbewahrend
unzulässig.

Brot als Göttergabe In Ägypten
wurde das Brot verehrt, wie kein
anderes Nahrungsmittel, die das
Gäge noch von Göttergabe Isis
und Osiris das Mahlzeiten geschenkt wurde. Der Teig wurde
von den Sklaven mit den Füßen
gestampft. Diese Sitte hielt sich
nach lange Zeit bis heute in reitagene Teile Europas, wie z.B.
Schweizrot. Durch den Fund einer
Hottgewerks im Grab. Kommen das
ihr weiß man heute genau, wie die
Ägypter ihren Bäckereien und
ihre Produkte ausgehen.

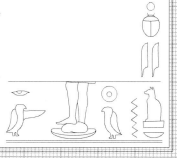

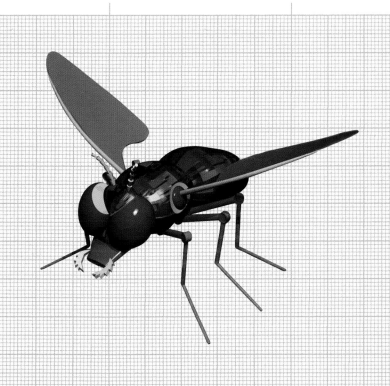

Illustrations are particularly well suited to
technical-scientific contents. They allow things to
be shown that are otherwise beyond the visible
range, or only exist in visual models.

Icons and Micons

The use of icons lends itself within a digital layout wherever a fact, characteristic or a function needs to be conveyed in a precise way. They are small visual signs that can make do without a lot of explanation and that allow for a space-saving organisation of an interface and the contents. In graphical terms, icons with a high iconicity are differentiated from those with a low iconicity. The full potential of icons may be seen when they are used in their dynamic form. Then they no longer appear simply as illustrations, but also as processes: sequences and actions are shown over time.

Low iconicity...

Abstract symbol
Has absolutely no representational quality. Is mainly based on conventions that first need to be learned.

Abstract representation
Has a representational quality, yet much simplified. Colour coding has no relation to reality.

Simple representation
The diagram is orientated towards reality; internal structures and a coloured design facilitate recognition. Simple plasticity by hinting at three-dimensionality.

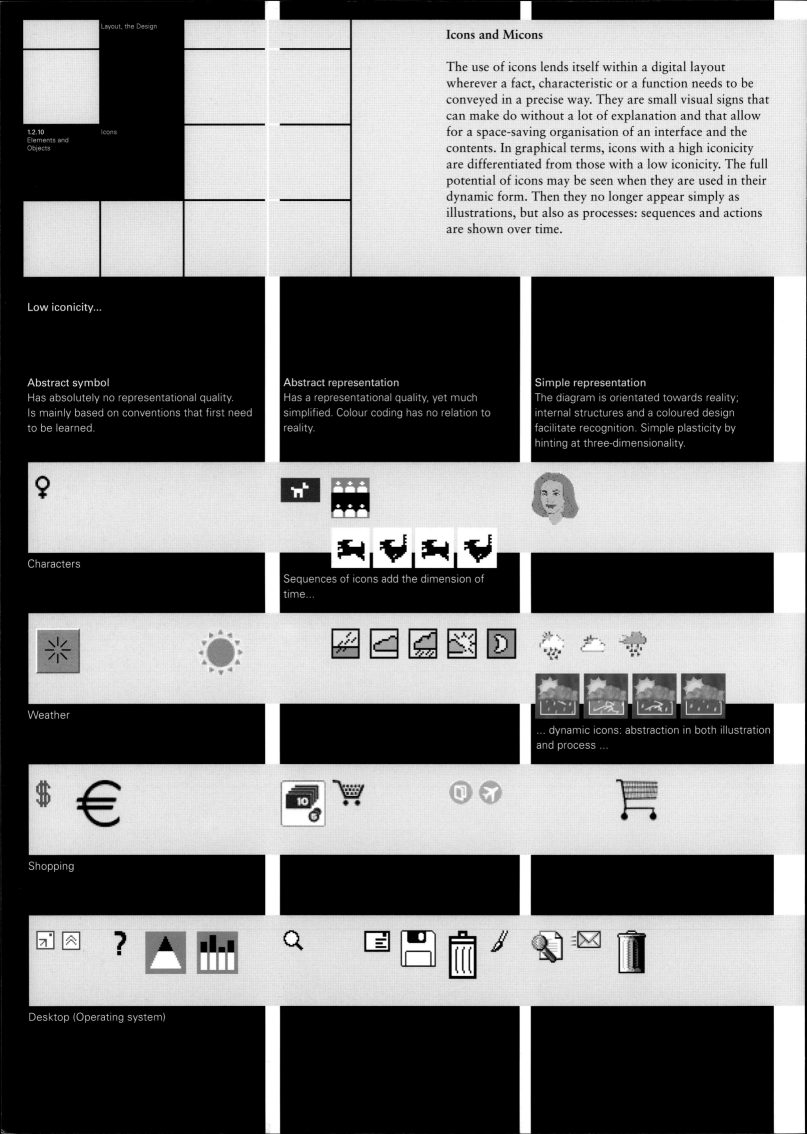

Characters

Sequences of icons add the dimension of time...

Weather

... dynamic icons: abstraction in both illustration and process ...

Shopping

Desktop (Operating system)

The higher the iconicity, the closer the sign is to reality and, conversely, with less iconicity the sign becomes more abstract. Since the introduction of graphical user interfaces icons have gradually progressed from a level of low iconicity towards higher iconicity, that is to say with a more detailed and more photorealistic quality. This is certainly due to the general increased performance of the hardware used: larger monitors, higher resolutions, more colours, faster image processing. And no doubt our perceptive habits in using digital media have also developed; from the initial steps in a new world of media right up to tools in our daily lives, with almost real attributes and corresponding, near real-time processing speeds.

With regard to digital layouts the question of the iconicity of icons becomes decisive once it becomes necessary to define how much space is available. Icons with a high pictorial quality require a higher resolution so as to allow the details to be reproduced exactly. Correspondingly, where there is too little space and resolution available, more abstract icons are better suited.

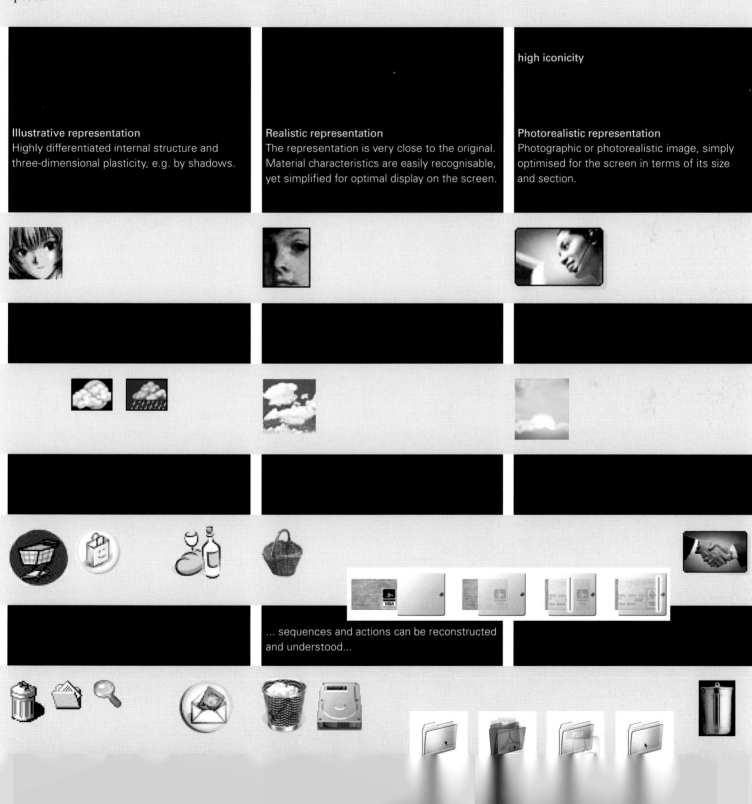

high iconicity

Illustrative representation
Highly differentiated internal structure and three-dimensional plasticity, e.g. by shadows.

Realistic representation
The representation is very close to the original. Material characteristics are easily recognisable, yet simplified for optimal display on the screen.

Photorealistic representation
Photographic or photorealistic image, simply optimised for the screen in terms of its size and section.

... sequences and actions can be reconstructed and understood...

Icons form an autonomous graphical unit in digital layouts, which ideally are in harmony with the overall image – in any case consistent in their visual language. The size and graphical implementation need to follow uniform rules and so make an icon identifiable as such and recognisable.

To this end, icons are often given characteristics to separate them from the rest of the interface, for example by way of plasticity, frames or other graphical codes. Similarly, the positioning plays a decisive role, which, where possible, is to be limited to pre-defined positions and chosen so as to be quickly understood.

Apart from the aspects of the visual presentation, the meaning of an icon within the digital layout also plays an important role. In this respect, icons may be divided into

Descriptive icon — The representation shows what it means and what significance it has, e.g. the hard drive that looks like a hard disk and stands for the computer's storage medium.

Informative function
Icons used simply for identification, representation or for information.

bbc.co.uk Weather forecast

The icons in a layout may well stem from 3 different groups with different meanings (index, metaphor, symbol). Yet in terms of their functional characteristics they have to be clearly differentiated: by way of their representation and/or position. In this series of examples this is achieved by different colours.

bertelsmann-club.de
Rating
Books
Computer accessories
Games
Personal promotion

belizeforum.com
Smile
Frown
Embarrass
Wink
Mad
Eek!

Activating function
The icon identifies an object or a button, which, when selected, then triggers an event or an interaction.

Print

amazon.com
Electronics
Home/crafts
Toys
Books
Travel
Computer games

MacOSX Hard drive

three basic groups: firstly, icons with pictorial characteristics, that is to say they show what is meant; for example a cloud to show the onset of clouds on the weather map. Secondly, icons with metaphoric characteristics, showing a figurative picture to stand for some other factual idea; for example, the trashcan showing the deleting of files. And, finally, the third group of symbolic icons, whose meaning first needs to be learnt, but ideally are based on standardised, well-known symbols; for example the cursor arrow that points to something and is really the representation of our hand.

When working on a digital layout an unmistakable assignment of icons to the groups named above is not always possible and not altogether necessary.

However, it does make sense to check that icons do not only have, for example, symbolic characteristics, since this could lead to a confusing user navigation system. On the other hand, it will be almost impossible to realise a concept of consistently pictorial icons, since numerous processes and functions in digital media have no real visualisation.

In digital layouts icons basically take on two different tasks: some are used as labels to inform, and are not directly linked to an interactive function. Others, however, trigger a direct action by clicking or moving, such as, for example, printing out a page or navigating through an application. In terms of optimal user-friendliness both these groups should be clearly differentiated by way of their design and/or position.

Metaphoric icon — The representation may show something real, but it means something else. The picture is used figuratively, e.g. the trashcan standing for the deletion of files.

Symbolic icon — A representation that is based on a generally understood convention. Otherwise the icon would be incomprehensible or its meaning would have to be first learnt in context.

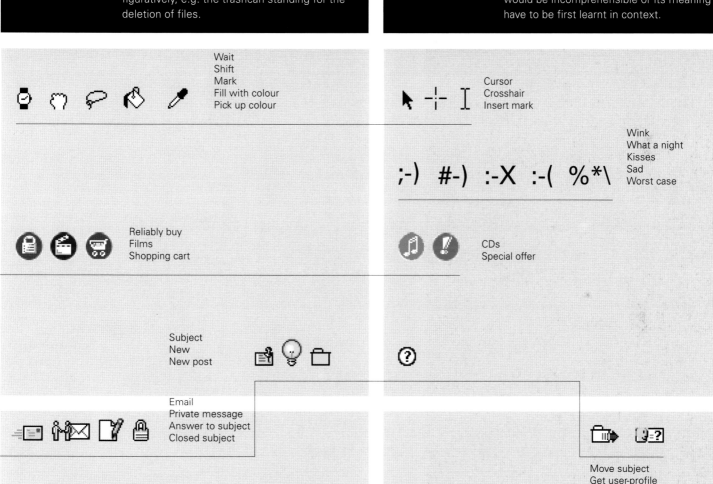

Wait
Shift
Mark
Fill with colour
Pick up colour

Cursor
Crosshair
Insert mark

;-) #-) :-X :-(%*\

Wink
What a night
Kisses
Sad
Worst case

Reliably buy
Films
Shopping cart

CDs
Special offer

Subject
New
New post

Email
Private message
Answer to subject
Closed subject

Move subject
Get user-profile

Show cart
Add to cart

Start action/go to
Dvd
Music

Trash   mail

Messenger

Functional elements

Functional elements are the most common way of turning the digital layout into an interface. They allow actions to be triggered, contents and objects to be worked on, navigation across several screens and much more. Two types of functional elements are used in digital layouts: the standardised functional elements taken from the "toolbox" belonging to the operating system; and functional elements, which are separately designed graphical elements, and whose functional characteristic is defined by relevant programming. Or to put it another way, the first group may be characterised as "practical" and the second as "individual".

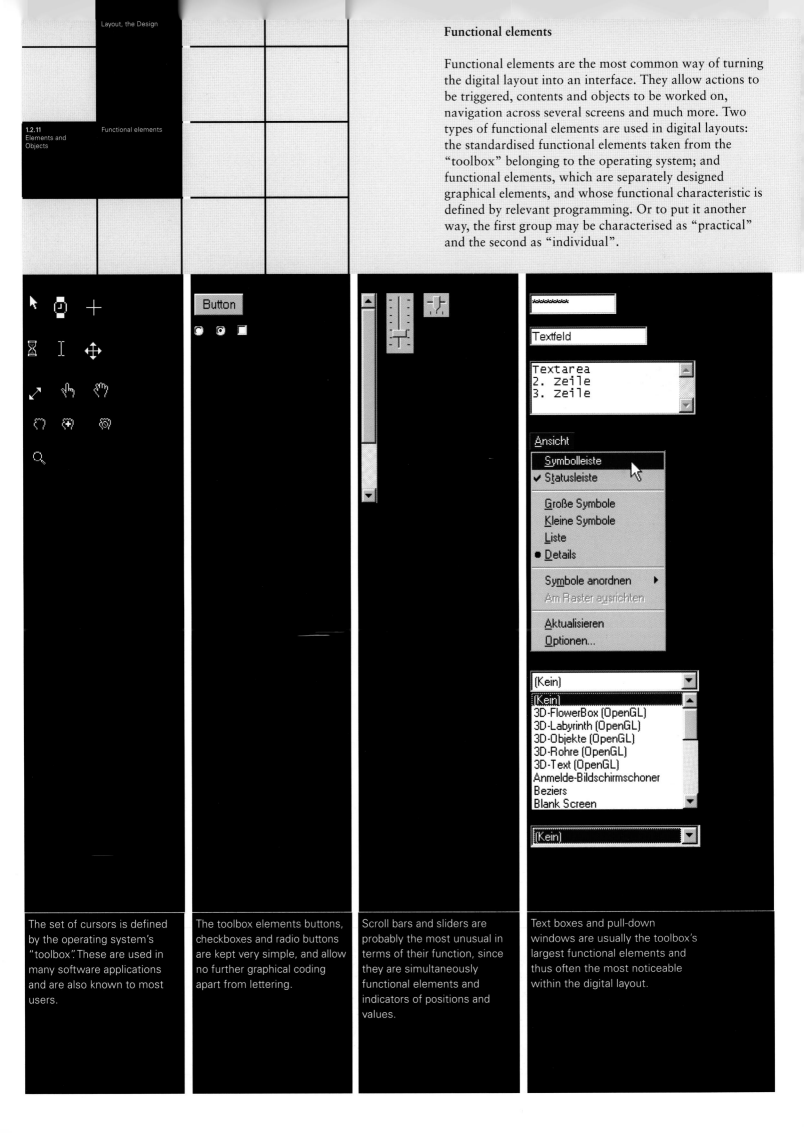

The set of cursors is defined by the operating system's "toolbox". These are used in many software applications and are also known to most users.

The toolbox elements buttons, checkboxes and radio buttons are kept very simple, and allow no further graphical coding apart from lettering.

Scroll bars and sliders are probably the most unusual in terms of their function, since they are simultaneously functional elements and indicators of positions and values.

Text boxes and pull-down windows are usually the toolbox's largest functional elements and thus often the most noticeable within the digital layout.

The toolbox's functional elements can technically be readily incorporated into the interface. They are found in many digital applications and thus are spontaneously understood by the users. Within the image, they speak the visual language of the operating system, are usually highlighted in 3D, and can hardly be altered and thus often seem somewhat out of place in a digital layout. Ideally these functional elements should be integrated, providing the differences in the image – for example, in terms of colour schemes and shapes – are not too extreme.

In design terms, individual functional elements can be much more easily integrated within the layout, but are more difficult to realise. They make an interface look harmonious and allow a homogenous relationship between content and function. This artistic freedom does have its limits, however, because what looks entirely logical at the design stage, may ultimately completely puzzle users. Thus it also makes sense to consider tried-and-tested functions – at least where standardised functions are to be represented by individual functional elements.

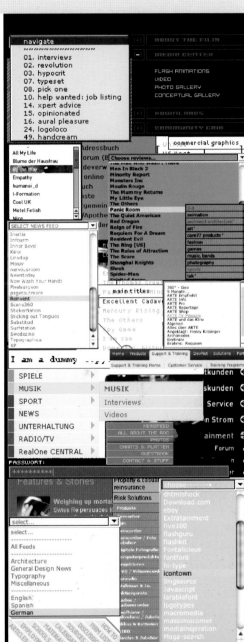

Individual cursors may be particularly useful if rollover with the mouse is to point out certain contents or functions.

Buttons and triggers of all kinds as individual elements are the easiest to realise and also the most common components of digital layouts.

Because of their unconventional functioning, in the case of individual scroll bars and sliders it is worthwhile going back to well-known functional principles.

Due to their format, text boxes and pull-down windows have a large influence on the overall image. Their individual matching to the layout is particularly obvious.

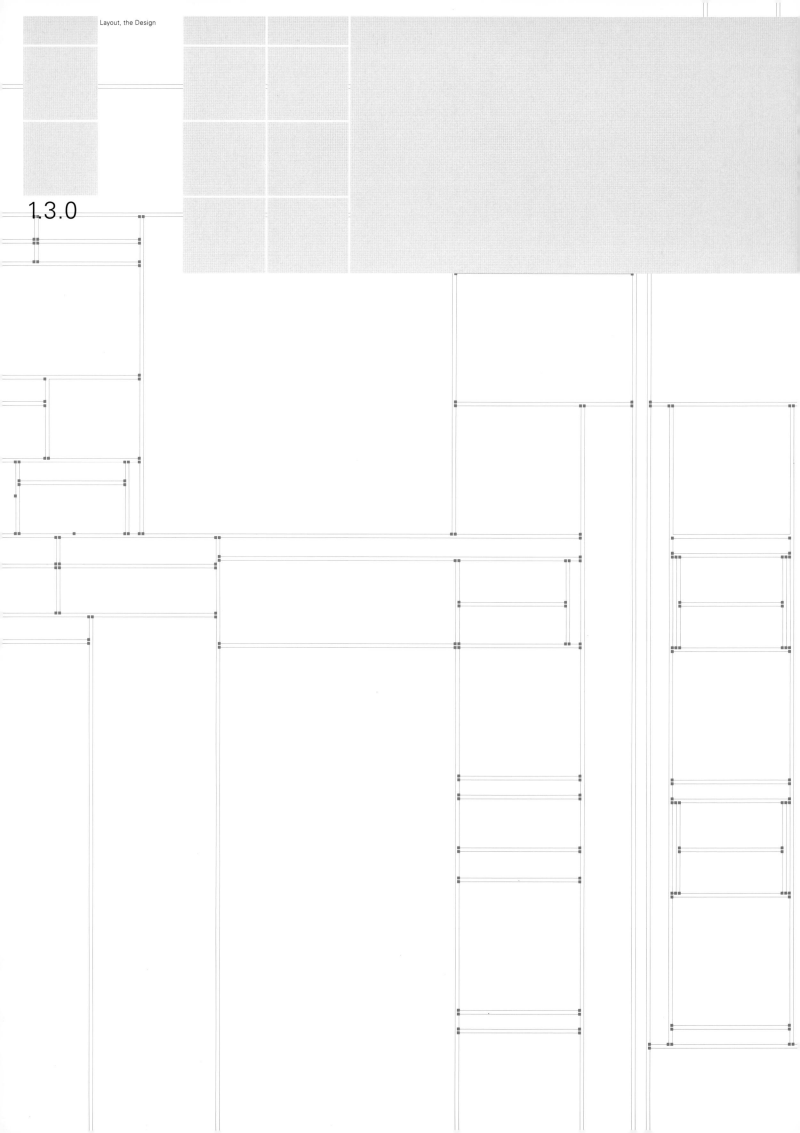

1.3.0

Montage

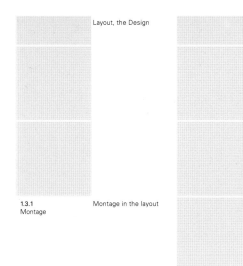

Montage in the layout

In terms of layout design, the term "montage" means both the piecing together of individual visual elements to form a new, significant image, as well as the technical aspect of montage: the joining together of individual components to form a technically constructed object. In the case of the digital layout this very aptly describes the functional character of an interface. Yet in visual design the term "montage" is unthinkable without the artistic forms of expression coined by such pioneers as Hans Richter, Sergei Eisenstein and Oskar Fischinger at the beginning of the 20th century.

Montage – like the sound of a symphony

A montage may refer to a single moment in time or a process over time.
Sergei Eisenstein[>1.3.2] refers to this as vertical and horizontal montage, that is to say the simultaneous (vertical) arrangement of elements and their chronological (horizontal) process. Eisenstein compared this to the score of a symphony, where the instruments are shown vertically and the sequence of the sounds horizontally.

Time-based software

This is the very principle found in the field of digital media when working in layers and arranging individual layout elements along the time axis: common computer programs are designed exactly according to this principle.

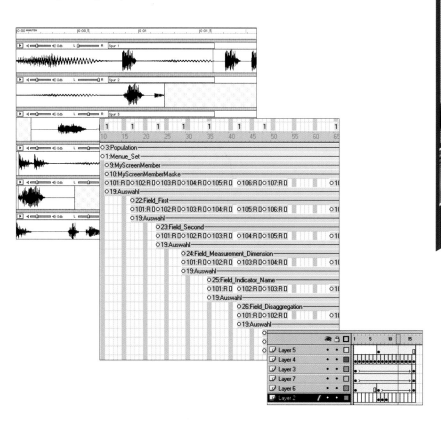

They assembled text, picture and sound elements to form collages and, by incorporating the dimension of time, created innovative forms of experimental film[>1.3-1]. The components used in these montages did not necessarily have to be directly interrelated; they only made sense after a certain amount of intellectual effort on the part of the observer.

Each element within the digital layout is determined by program code. Either individually or combined to form groups, they create figures, which are largely flexible in their position and shape. During the montage process of a layout they may be freely moved, built up in layers, duplicated, scaled up or down, altered in their appearance – and then returned to their original state. Digital layouts are modularly constructed and ideally they should remain modular – as opposed to the layout of classical media, where the graphical elements in the final product enter into a solid, unalterable relationship with the information medium. This basic difference leads to digital media linking static and dynamic types of montage and allows layout concepts, whose origins are equally found in the design fundamentals of film and print media.

Technical montage
The piecing together of individual elements that results in a functional object – montage here means a technical process, as it is also known in the field of communication media. Within the layout, too, individual elements are joined together to form an image that may take on the function of a man-machine interface.

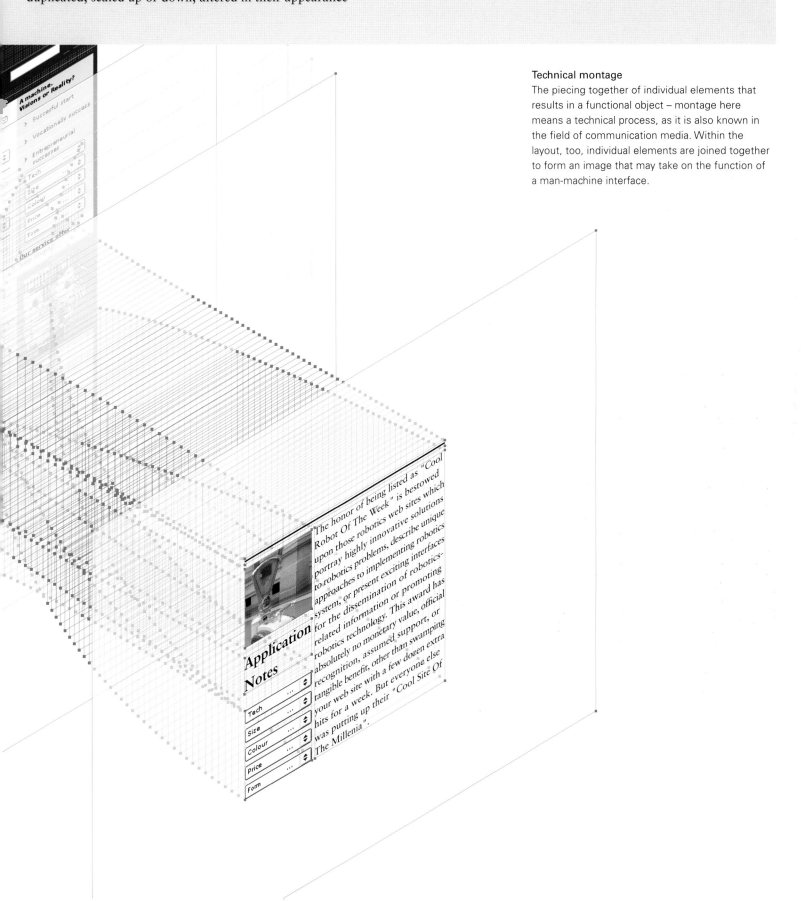

Vertical montage – figure-ground

Graphical elements – individual or in groups – form figures, which are positioned in relation to the ground. In this way, the figures and the ground considerably influence each other: each alteration to the figure's position also changes the impression made by the ground, which within the digital layout corresponds to the "window", for example. The aim in designing the figure-ground relationship is to promote the perception of the figures, convey a certain layout character and organise the interaction with the interface. Where this process is applied to an individual situation it corresponds to the principle of "vertical montage", and may be constructed according to formal and semantic criteria.

Formal figure-ground relations

The positioning follows certain rules, aimed at representing a particular form:

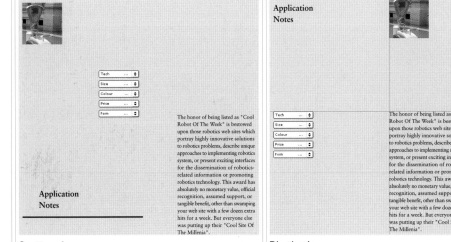

Centred
Positioned in the middle of the composition.

Tense
Very close to the edge on the one hand, so as to produce as large an area as possible on the other.

Harmonious
The classical arrangement of the "golden ratio" with a ratio of 1:1:6.

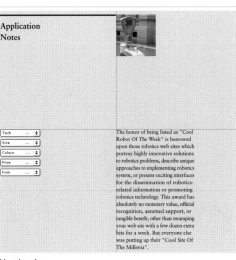
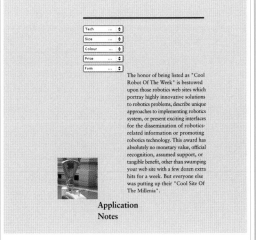

Scattered
Completely random positioning.

Rhythmic
The individual elements are positioned at recurring, identical distances.

Figurative
Forming a "5".

Vertical montages aimed at creating a figure-ground relation may be distinguished according to two principles: a montage following formal rules is free of contextual meaning and is thus useful as a design guideline on a very basic level. This leads to hard and fast rules for determining a positional relation, such as "always align centrally". This is different with semantic criteria, which mainly refer to the meaning resulting from a montage. A simple example of this is that the "most important" things are right at the top. Managing the visual impression using the figure-ground relation is a very effective principle in layout design. It serves as the basis for syntactic rules determining the montage design for a whole series of layouts.

Semantic figure-ground relation

The positioning is orientated towards the meaning that is to be conveyed:

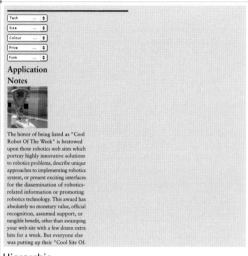

Hierarchic
The position results from the importance of the element, independent of the reading habits.

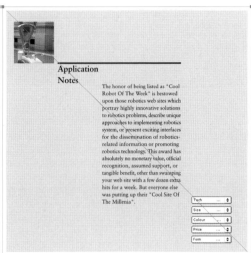

Linear
Here the ordering corresponds to possible reading habits, facilitating comprehension of the contents.

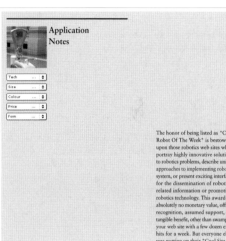

Weighted
The photograph is the central topic and everything is positioned around this so as to underline its significance.

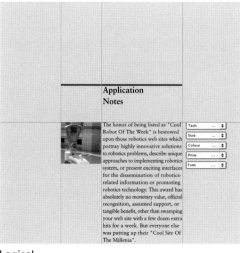

Logical
The entire image should convey the contextual links between the elements themselves.

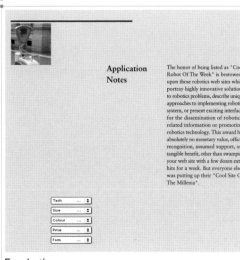

Emphatic
The entire image should use empty space to highlight the autonomous role of the individual elements.

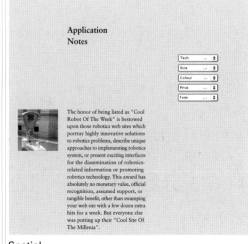

Spatial
Comprehensive, more complex elements are placed below, the more simple ones further up, resulting in a "spatial" structuring.

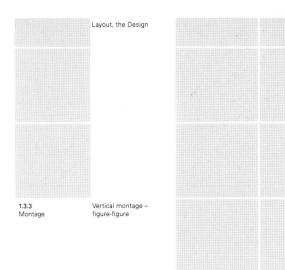

Vertical montage – figure-figure

The relationships between the figures themselves form the basis for an ordering system, as is necessary for decoding an interface. The digital layout unites different components in a confined space, whose functional characteristics may already be labelled by way of the spatial structuring. For example, do the buttons apply to a selection of different images or to different texts? Does the interaction cause a partial change, or does it change the entire contents of the window? Here the spatial ordering alone provides more and clearer indications than would be possible using words.

Changing relationships

There are no doubt countless ways of creating relationships between individual figures (in this case elements). Some of them are very simple, yet extremely effective:

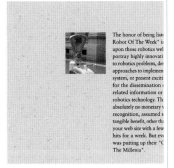

Space

Using space to link and separate. Two things standing close together are understood as belonging together. Distance, on the other hand, creates an idea of separation – even in the case of just a few elements.

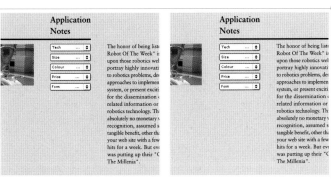

Alignment

Simple graphical elements, such as the line here, create transparency. The buttons in the middle correspond to the picture on the left and to the text on the right. Just the line on its own alters the meaning of the elements – which can considerably simplify the layout of an interface.

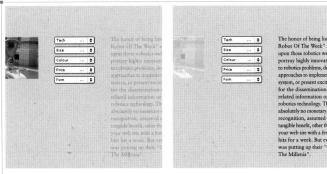

Presence

The presence of individual elements can also convey a sense of interconnection – even countering the structural effect of other elements.

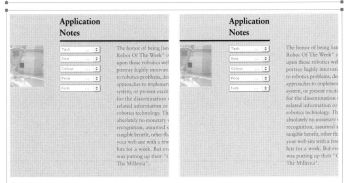

Coding

As well as colour coding, which clearly shows a sense of interconnection.

Let us return to the advantages of the montage within the digital layout. The technical independence of individual elements allows their appearance to be modified without having to depart from the current environment. This means changing relationships and orders can be shown in the interface, which are completely adapted to the current situation and help users to retain an overview. The overlapping of individual elements also takes on a new meaning here. In the figure-base area as well as in the figure-figure relation a spatial impression is quickly created, which may be used as a further ordering system.

The relationship between the elements also decides the "spatial" order. Even the simplest changes to the intensity or size of the illustration directly affect the spatial impression. Light-dark, large-small. Virtual space is based on human experience without actually having to be three-dimensional. > 3.2

Intensifying and emphasising

The technical independence of individual elements allows different types of emphasis, such as over-lapping in layers or scaling. By using intensification the structure may be varied and its coding modified. This allows active and inactive elements to be labelled and hierarchies to be displayed. Scaling individual elements is most certainly the easiest and most obvious type of emphasis.

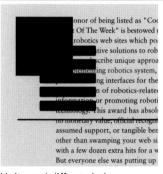
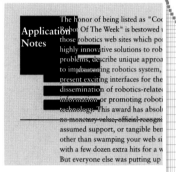
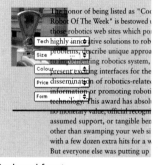
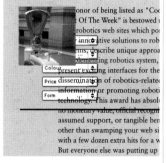

Unity and differentiation

The uniform colouring dissolves the differentiation and allows the different elements and layers to melt into one figure on one layer. A mutual blank space highlights the individual parts, while retaining the impression of a closed figure.

Back and front

The structure of the layers within the intensification alone represents a hierarchy. One of the main advantages of the digital layout is that the arrangement can be flexibly designed. It is not in the least determined whether an element is placed at the front or the back, but may be dynamically altered.

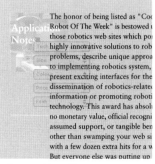
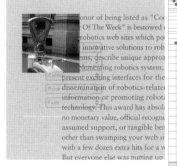

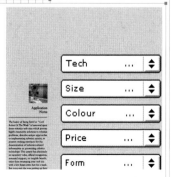

Active and inactive

A uniform gradation allows intensified elements to blend into the background, so that individual elements may be highlighted using their original tonal value. All the elements remain present and yet may be differentiated in terms of their significance – so as to label them as active or inactive, for example.

Large and small

This is without doubt the simplest and most obvious way of showing the status of individual elements.

Horizontal montage – figure-ground-time

Horizontal montage and film editing represent the same process: the joining together of images or image sequences in a chronological order. Yet, as opposed to film, with the montage of a digital layout the technical independence of the individual elements may be largely retained. Thus, parts of the layout may follow a dynamic movement or change, while others are simply integrated in their static form – and this may be completely reversed the next time.

Hard cut
The alterations to the image are abrupt. Complete changes are easier to perceive than partial ones, such as a simple change of position.

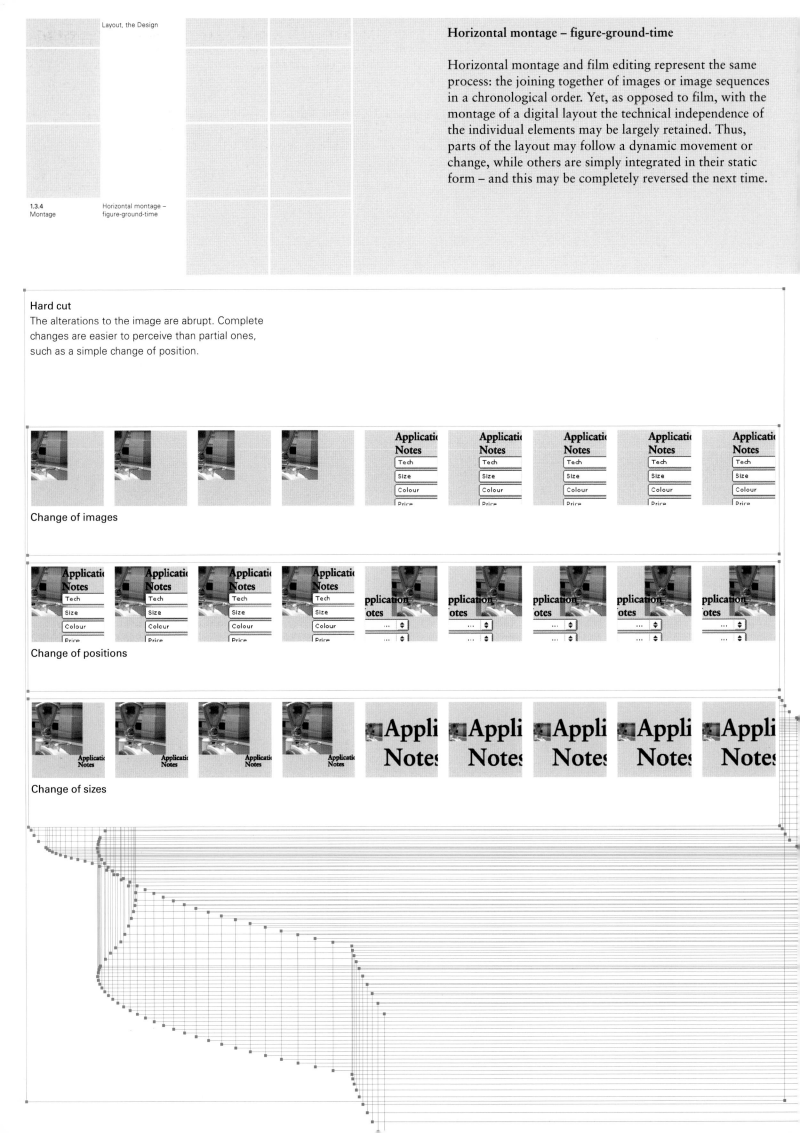

Change of images

Change of positions

Change of sizes

The technical and syntactic principles in horizontal montage correspond to those of film editing and are divided into "hard" and "soft" cuts. Digital media allow this to happen in multiple ways and at the same time: with regard to the entire layout, or limited to individual elements and areas. Thus, Sergei Eisenstein's comparison of montage in film with the score of an orchestral piece of music[>1.3-1] applies all the more to the digital layout. Here, too, the aim is to precisely "compose" the interplay between the elements into a visual, time-based montage.

Apart from the filmic presentation of contents, animated sequences also help to organise the components within a layout. For example, parts that are only needed temporarily can be faded in and out as required, their size and appearance altered or their position changed. "Hard-cut" transformations demand more of the user's attention than "soft" ones. Due to the complexity of many interfaces it is thus often very useful to design alterations as intelligible animated sequences.

Soft cut

Changes occur smoothly, with several intermittent cuts. These may be structured continuously, but also so as to accelerate or slow down the movement.

Smooth movement

Soft dissolve

Morphing

Wiping, twisting

Fading in

Visual gestures

Gestures are forms of expression that are registered in their entirety, and that accompany the actual dissemination of information by way of texts or images. The result of a montage, too, may be termed a visual gesture, which is largely decisive for the overall appearance of the layout. Visual gestures help to convey the impression, without having to explicitly refer to it, for example in the text. This is decisive wherever a differentiated observation of the different levels of meaning in a layout is concerned, where contents, impressions and possible interactions need to be clearly identifiable without long explanations.

Denotation
Objective description

Line and image

Application Notes

The honor of being listed as "Cool Robot Of The Week" is bestowed upon those robotics web sites which portray highly innovative solutions to robotics problems, describe unique approaches to implementing robotics system, or present exciting interfaces for the dissemination of robotics-related information or promoting robotics technology. This award has absolutely no monetary value, official recognition, assumed support, or tangible benefit, other than swamping your web site with a few dozen extra hits for a week. But everyone else was putting up their "Cool Site Of The Millenia".

Headline and text

Buttons (trigger menu)

Connotation
Associative description

The layout appears tidy and accessible. All three groups seem to refer to the whole situation, while the text appears to play an important role due to its size. It is obvious that clicking on the buttons will affect the entire contents.

Application Notes

The honor of being listed as "Cool Robot Of The Week" is bestowed upon those robotics web sites which portray highly innovative solutions to robotics problems, describe unique approaches to implementing robotics system, or present exciting interfaces for the dissemination of robotics-related information or promoting robotics technology. This award has absolutely no monetary value, official recognition, assumed support, or tangible benefit, other than swamping your web site with a few dozen extra hits for a week. But everyone else was putting up their "Cool Site Of The Millenia".

Semiotic aspects

Syntactic level
The five elements form three groups. Their ordering makes recurring use of the axes of the individual elements. The empty space takes on a dividing function here. The image and line are in the upper part, the text element in the middle and the functional elements in the lower part.

Application Notes

The honor of being listed as "Cool Robot Of The Week" is bestowed upon those robotics web sites which portray highly innovative solutions to robotics problems, describe unique approaches to implementing robotics system, or present exciting interfaces for the dissemination of robotics-related information or promoting robotics technology. This award has absolutely no monetary value, official recognition, assumed support, or tangible benefit, other than swamping your web site with a few dozen extra hits for a week. But everyone else was putting up their "Cool Site Of The Millenia".

Semantic level
The impression created by the layout is rather open and reserved, appears inviting, friendly and wide. It looks casual and neutral, full of variety and familiar. It is certainly lively, somewhat vibrant, but maybe a little conventional...

Pragmatic level
First the image, and then? The buttons appear important, but the headline and text come first. What does the image show? Perhaps we should first read the text. Aha, the image refers to the text. And the buttons? What are my choices here? Let's read on. Click here. Yes, that sounds interesting. Click.

In terms of its message a layout is always multi-layered: it contains a denotative level, which objectively describes the matter, as well as a connotative level, which refers to the field of association in its appearance.

Taken semiotically – that is to say in terms of physical experience – there are three further aspects: a syntactic level, which defines the formal relations among the layout components, and a semantic level, from which the impression made by the layout is derived. Finally, the pragmatic level includes the direct actions, resulting from the analysis of the layout.

In objectively observing a layout the semantic aspects offer the greatest scope for interpretation. This is why a "semantic differential" is often used to evaluate the impression made by a layout. This serves to measure the meaning of different means of expression and was developed as early as 1957 by the psychologists Osgood, Suci and Tannenbaum [1.3-2]. A series of opposing terms allows an objective evaluation of the strongly subjective perception of a layout. This is most successful when the intentions of the layout are defined using the same "semantic differential" prior to starting the design process.

	-3	-2	-1	0	1	2	3	
exciting									relaxing
liberating									inhibiting
calming									frightening
inviting									repulsive
uniform									unpredictable
emotional									neutral
near									far
friendly									unfriendly
heavy									light
harmonious									unbalanced
hard									soft
innovative									conventional
cold									warm
lively									rigid
monotonous									varied
open									closed
quiet									vibrant
vibrant									organic
understandable									incomprehensible
familiar									strange
reticent									pushy

Seven-layer, semantic differential
A semantic differential is made up of a series of opposing terms. These are mainly adjectives, which describe polarised impressions. There is no definite rule for the choice of terms, but ideally they should be orientated towards the characteristics that a design needs to contain. Similarly, the number of pairs is not determined – usually around 20. The original invented by Osgood, Suci and Tannenbaum [1.3-2], incidentally, used just 12. The semantic differential may be used for an objective evaluation of the subjective impression made by a design.

To determine the semantic differential a scale from −3 to +3 is used between the terms. This may also be used to define the aims before starting work on the actual design phase. This evaluation should be carried out with several candidates, whose results are then compared to the desired profile. This prevents very vague evaluations of the visual impression and provides pointers to the deviations from the desired result.

2.1.0

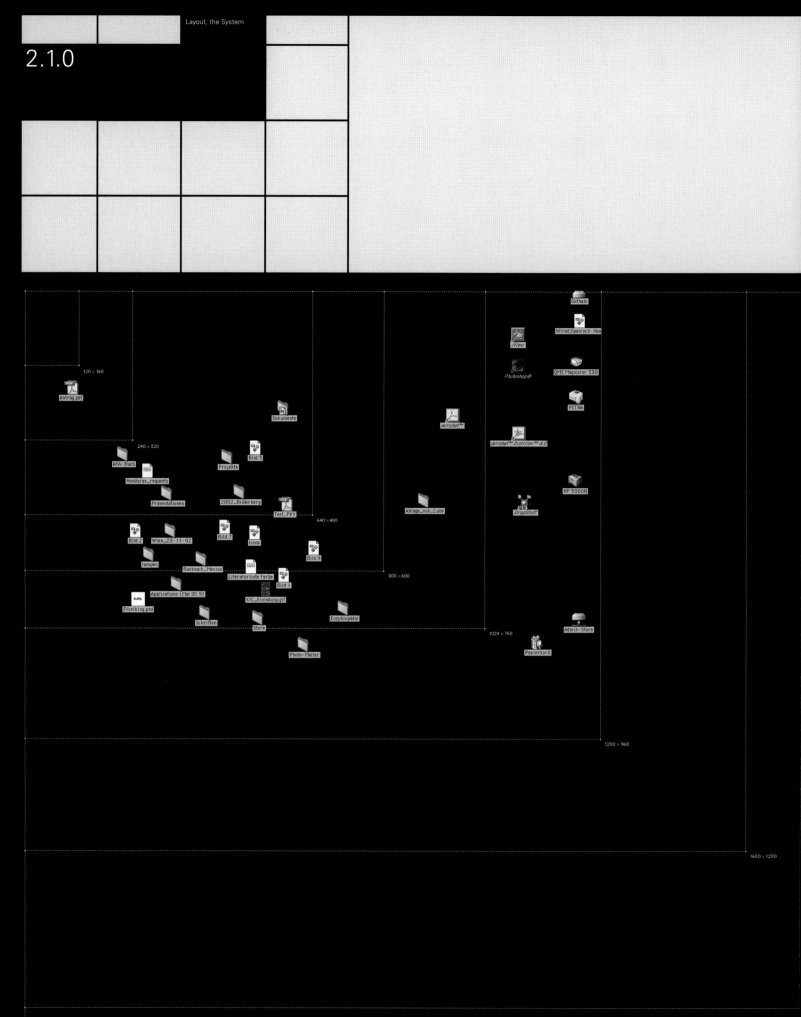

120 × 160

Antrag.pdf

240 × 320

AYA-Buch

Honduras_requests

Präsentationen

Dokumente

Bild 3

Projekte

2002_Bilderberg

Test_PKY

640 × 480

Bild 2   Wien_23-11-02

Bild 7

Icons

Bild 9

Lampen

Rucksack_Mexico

Literaturliste Farbe   Bild 1

Applications (Mac OS 9)

Pixelking.psd

KJC_Einladung.gif

Schriften

Store

Enzyklopädie

Photo-Mailer

800 × 600

Ablage_von_Cube

Acrobat™

Acrobat™ Distiller™ 4.0

Gotham

Wired.Spanisch-Hea

iView

Photoshop®

QMS Magicolor 330

PETRA

HP 5000N

DropStuff

1024 × 768

Admin-Store

Papierkorb

1280 × 960

1600 × 1200

Formats

Compared to classical media, layout formats within
the digital scope of action are often designed horizontally.
This usually corresponds to the hardware used, since a
large number of displays use landscape mode. In light
of the historical precursors of film and television, the
development of the horizontal media format appears to be
obvious. Yet experts tend to assume that the development
of the computer display stems from that of military radar.
A horizontal display format, that of the "window on the
digital world", does indeed allow a direct link to the user's
facial features – these are also horizontal, just like the
viewing and reading habits in most cultures. >3.2

Eyes
The face has a horizontal format and takes in a
horizontal field of 180 degrees and a vertical field
of 130 degrees, corresponding to a ratio of
approximately 3:2.

Newspaper
Landscape, portrait, landscape
– a newspaper folded at a
kiosk, showing the front page
and an opened out double-page
spread of the interior. Here is
a medium with different format
variations, which are also
treated correspondingly in
the design.

Print formats
The standardisation of print
formats facilitates the technical
production of print media.
The series of DIN formats
commonly used in Europe is
designed so as to allow all
formats to be derived from one
basic format and to additionally
retain the same proportions
throughout.

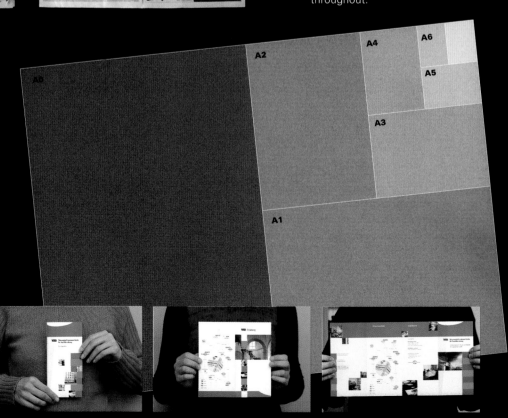

Flyer
Small, handy, surprising. The
scope for development with
printed matter allows for a
varied design and variation
of the format, which always
retains its contextual interde-
pendencies due to the folding
and binding even in a changeable context.

On the other hand, wherever ergonomic reasons have resulted in a vertical display, such as with handhelds or mobile telephones, for example, the result is autonomous formatted rows on the display.

However, the horizontal layout format of the display is not in any way pre-defined. The arrangement of different windows on the basic display level allows as wide a range of possibilities as found in classical media, where the format and design are aligned with the purpose, contents, production and handling. And, as the example of the folding of printed matter shows, even variations of differing formats are possible within one medium, with corresponding variations in the preparation of the layout design.

The principle behind the representation of applications in separate windows – such as with websites or software – allows the simultaneous representation of several windows of varying sizes on the display. However, the whole of the display may also be used, if, for example, there is not enough room for other windows or only one application is to be made available. In such cases, the digital layout is orientated towards the features of the display. And more besides: even the characteristics of the display, such as its proportions or the plastic casing, can considerably influence the layout – and the more an application is designed for a particular type of display, the more this needs to be considered when designing the layout. >3.1

Picture tubes
The very first picture tubes (Ferdinand Braun, Manfred von Ardenne) used in television sets showed a horizontal layout, just like cinema films – analogous to the human face.

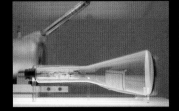

Display formats
Display formats and resolutions develop in line with technical progress, and thus are becoming increasingly numerous. But at least with the proportions (4:3) there appears to be some consistency. Exceptions among individual display types or laptops prove the rule. Similarly, in the development of mobile devices at least one proportion (3:4) seems to be predominant. Yet nearly all displays have one thing in common: the number 8 as the largest common denominator in display resolution, that is to say the universal number when it comes to pixel sizes in a digital layout.

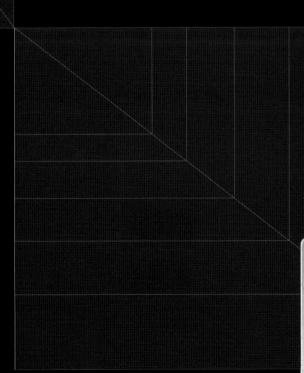

Monitors
Using the entire display produces a horizontal layout shape, while working within windows allows different layouts and sizes. The separation of applications into multiple windows allows for the multilevel and simultaneous presentation of information sources and tools on the computer.

Format typology

The contents of a digital application may be organised into windows in different ways; the basis of the digital layout. Here, they may be edited within a single page in one continuous window, spread over several hyperlinked pages inside a window or even over several pages in parallel windows. Separation within one page makes particular demands of the layout, since it usually contains more contents than is originally visible in the window and than is normally expected from a document. Here, graphical orientation elements and structures aid navigation by scrolling or jumping.

One window, all the contents
Whoever has a lot of contents on offer will have great difficulties with this principle. Even if scrolling is considered normal, the organisation of all the contents in one window prevents an overview. It makes more sense to divide up the contents according to subject and to offer them to users in well-structured portions.

One window, multiple contents
The standard in processing digital documents: Different contents are hyperlinked within one window and selected for display by the user. One window defines the standard frame where all the functions and contents are housed.

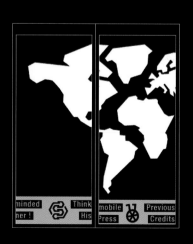

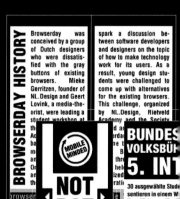

Longer passages of text, for example, should not only be structured in terms of their contents, but also in readily comprehensible units. In dividing up contents over several pages within one window, it is important to include the relevant page headers and coding. These help users recognise the fact that while the page has changed, the contextual contents are the same. As does the division of contents over several windows, although frowned upon by usability experts. This occurs mainly where the contents are used as an addition and are modular; for example, where the main window is extended using further, subordinate elements. It is important here that the windows are identified as being interrelated, since they face direct competition from other windows that may contain other applications, such as websites or programs.

The different possibilities for choosing the format and structuring documents necessitate a consistency within the visual language, that of the digital layout. A uniform definition of the design elements and a consistent structuring are indispensable for the successful use of digital applications. Even the most curious users are disappointed by experimental challenges if there is no visual consistency.

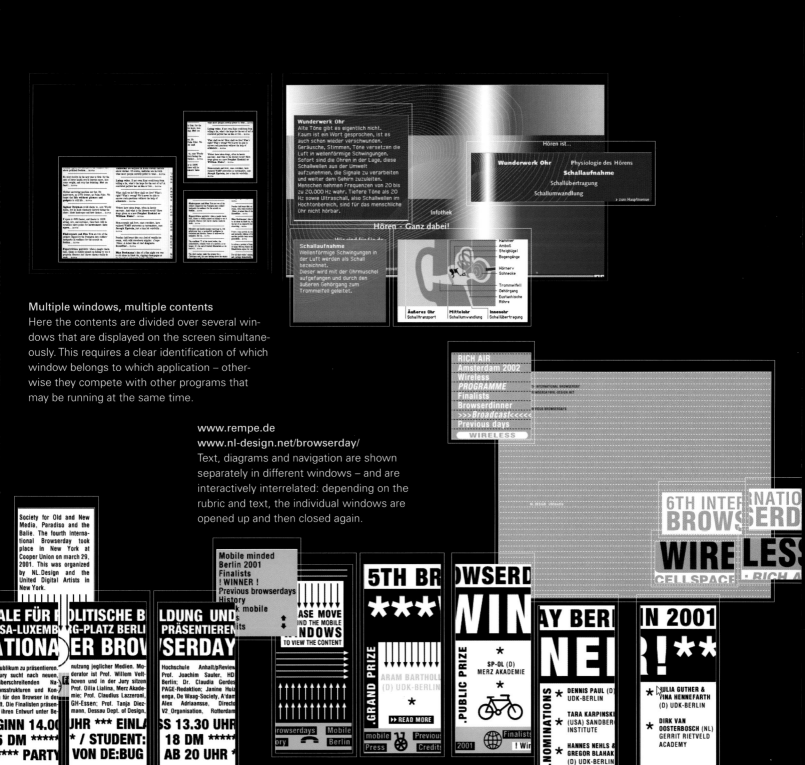

Multiple windows, multiple contents
Here the contents are divided over several windows that are displayed on the screen simultaneously. This requires a clear identification of which window belongs to which application – otherwise they compete with other programs that may be running at the same time.

www.rempe.de
www.nl-design.net/browserday/
Text, diagrams and navigation are shown separately in different windows – and are interactively interrelated: depending on the rubric and text, the individual windows are opened up and then closed again.

Content beyond the visible

Where the format reaches its limits in classical media
is where it becomes really exciting in digital layouts –
because, as opposed to the classical media, the preparation
of digital contents can include the invisible, virtual scope.
Learning the functions of a computer interface equips
practically every user with the knowledge of what a
virtual extension of the visible window's contents allows.

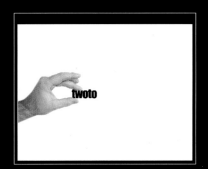

www.twoto.com
The classical principle of cropping used
in the browser window format: a hand reaches into the layout area and manipulates
other elements within the layout.

RICK MACARTHUR: Ladies and gentlemen, my name is Rick MacArthur and I
am the publisher of *Harper's Magazine*. On behalf of *Harper's* and the
National Endowment for the Humanities, I want to welcome you to this
gathering of teachers, administrators, cultural observers, and business and
government leaders, a symposium which we have ambitiously titled, "In
Search of the Educated American." Amid increasingly emotional national
debates about teacher shortages, school vouchers and standardized testing, a
critical question is generally overlooked: What is the purpose of an education
in America today? Is the purpose to get a job, get into college? Is it to create
reflective citizens who are capable of self-government, both in the realm of
politics and emotion? Is it to instruct students in the rules of society and in the
love of learning? Is it all of the above? And if it is, what is preventing us from
attaining those goals on a broader, more universal scale? Are we failing too
many of those Americans who would like to participate in our grand
democratic experiment, but for all sorts of reasons, cannot? We devoted
most of the special fall issue of *Harper's Magazine* to the subject and, in co-
sponsorship with the National Endowment for the Humanities, designed this
program to continue the conversation begun in the pages of the magazine. To
further introduce today's program, I'd like to present William Ferris,
Chairman of the NEH.

WILLIAM R. FERRIS: NEH's founding legislation states that democracy
demands wisdom, a mission and a message made all the more compelling by
the tragic events of September 11, exactly two weeks ago today. At times
like these, the humanities serve as a healing voice for all Americans. We find
solace in writers such as William Faulkner, who deeply believed that the
human spirit could rise above adversity and triumph. In his Nobel Prize
acceptance speech, he wrote, "I believe that man will not merely endure. He
will prevail. He is immortal, not because he alone among creatures has an
inexhaustible voice, but because he has a soul, a spirit capable of compassion
and sacrifice and endurance." His words ring true, as the events of
September 11 have now become part of our nation's history. I see in a way
this day as a kind of feast of ideas and a vision for the future of this great
nation. And who better to launch this first novel than Leura Lanham

Simple Text
The classic among format-breakers:
read, scroll, read, scroll …

Scrolling, moving or enlarging – contents at the edge of a window may be pushed into the picture in a number of ways. In the user's expectations, the cropping of a format within a digital layout basically means that the contents can be continued beyond the visible range. And if such hints as a scroll bar or a cursor-hand appear, then this is generally the case. On the other hand, disrupted typography or a cropped image that needs to be scrolled within the window can be frustrating.

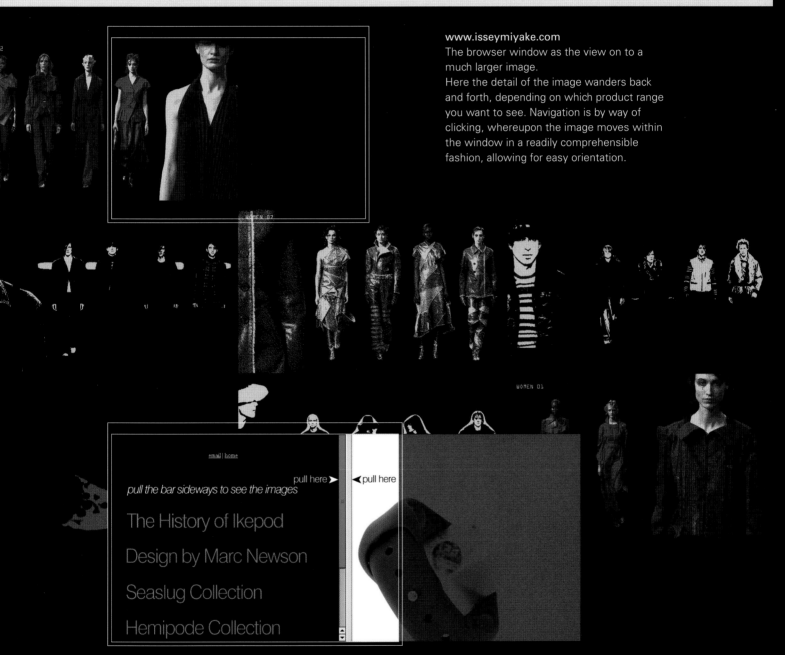

www.isseymiyake.com
The browser window as the view on to a much larger image.
Here the detail of the image wanders back and forth, depending on which product range you want to see. Navigation is by way of clicking, whereupon the image moves within the window in a readily comprehensible fashion, allowing for easy orientation.

www.ikepod.com
Limitations on the format can also be integrated into the layout design – as on the IKEPOD website. "Pull Here" – a variable division of the layout area allows the sections to be closed and opened up within the browser window.

Layout beyond the visible

Integrating the invisible in a digital layout need not necessarily be a contextual necessity, it could also be an interesting design element. Moving screen contents around then becomes a simple dramatic means, allowing an exciting or even a particularly apposite handling of contents. This type of layout is particularly well suited to time-based, sychronoptic representations or for narrative contents, where the linearity of the chronological process is analogous to the visible window section. This does, however, assume a corresponding handling of the layout: navigational aids, like button links, and orientation aids, such as position markers, are indispensable.

www.triquart-partner.de

Simple ideas can be very effective, and humorous. This series of Post-it® notes explains why this Web agency does not have a real website of its own. The horizontal space beyond the browser was simply integrated into the layout, and navigation is done by scrolling – which is all that is needed in this case.

Similarly the layout structure should be kept consistent, for example, on the basis of a continuous design grid, as well as in the "virtual" part. The principle of the virtual continuation of the layout should be instantly recognisable and be the uniform concept behind the entire application. A cropped layout is then not perceived so much as an incomplete image, but rather as a challenge to our powers of imagination; a method that consciously assumes curiosity and a love of experimentation on the part of the user.

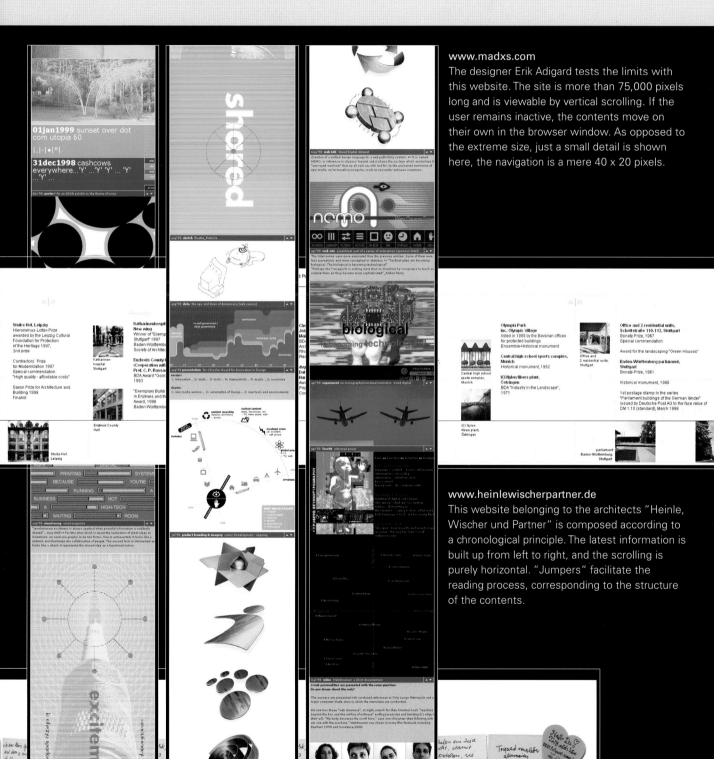

www.madxs.com

The designer Erik Adigard tests the limits with this website. The site is more than 75,000 pixels long and is viewable by vertical scrolling. If the user remains inactive, the contents move on their own in the browser window. As opposed to the extreme size, just a small detail is shown here, the navigation is a mere 40 x 20 pixels.

www.heinlewischerpartner.de

This website belonging to the architects "Heinle, Wischer und Partner" is composed according to a chronological principle. The latest information is built up from left to right, and the scrolling is purely horizontal. "Jumpers" facilitate the reading process, corresponding to the structure of the contents.

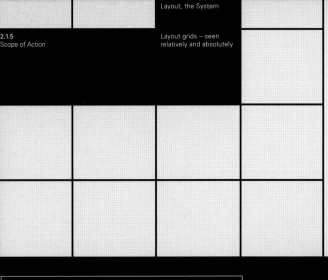

Layout grids – seen relatively and absolutely

If the layout of a digital application is to be based on a consistent structure, the use of a layout grid is indispensable. It aids a uniform structuring and defines the size and positions of all components of the layout area. An ordered structure need not be recognisable at first glance and yet in many cases it will form the basis of a layout – even if the definition of that which may be termed a layout grid differs widely. This may be seen in particular where the two different measuring systems in digital layouts are concerned: relative measurements, where all values are given in percentages or relative units, and absolute measurements, where all values are given absolutely in pixels.

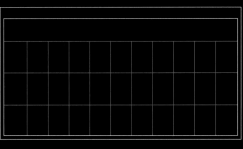

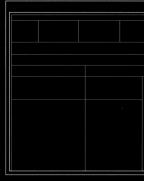

www.helmutlang.com
Professional websites that do completely without a layout grid are seldom found and even then, the lack of a layout grid is often a

www.sun.com
The Sun Microsystems website is structured completely using relative measurements and changes with each resizing of the browser

Relative measuring is based on the idea that sizes and positions can always be altered in relation to the window size, typeface and type size, and thus are always different depending on the user's settings. The idea behind absolute measuring is simply that the appearance of a layout is the same on all systems and the user cannot exert any influence. In the meantime, this has become a basic prerequisite for the modular structure of a layout as well as with database-supported systems >2.2, whose components are based on reliable sizes.

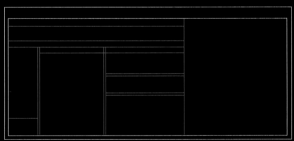

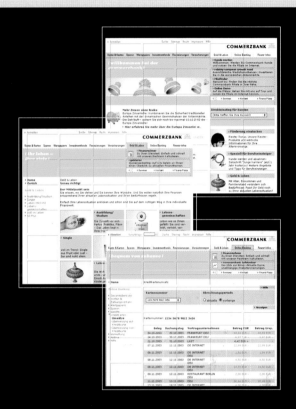

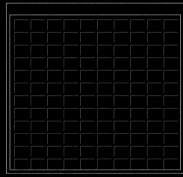

www.cnn.com
The CNN website clearly aims to appear the same on all systems and all over the world. Thus with particularly small browser windows only a section is visible, while particularly large windows display an empty window section. The layout grid corresponds to the axes resulting from the main components and columns.

www.commerzbank.de
This site also ensures that it looks the same on all systems – which is particularly crucial with online banking making heavy use of database relationships, since modular elements are constantly being exchanged, the size of which need to be determined in advance.
A layout grid also facilitates this modular way of working, using uniform units across the whole layout area. This provides concrete starting points for sizing and positioning the elements on the most varied types of page layout.

Structured flexibility

A consistently applied layout grid is always advantageous when dealing with structured work on the layout – indispensable with large-scale applications and a complex structuring of the interface. Only a uniform layout grid ensures that recurring questions of design need not be constantly resolved again and again and, in the worst-case scenario, leading to irritation in the perception and application of the interface. Seen in this light, a layout grid ensures a simplification of the design process and thus of the work involved. Only at first glance does a layout grid appear restrictive, since in practice it can be far more restricting during the design process to have to constantly produce new variations of the layout structure.

A layout grid using uniform units of size assumes the definition of a uniform measuring system. An absolute measuring system is logically based on the smallest unit of the display itself, the pixel, or a group of pixels. For a relative measurement, some programs for developing interfaces provide special measuring systems; for example, a "twip" that always displays 1/9600 of the current monitor resolution. However, other vector-based programs, such as Flash, allow the use of centimetres or inches, since in any case the layout area can be scaled up or down in a later application.

The design of a layout grid shown here is based on an absolute measurement in pixels, yet may be applied to other units of measurement.

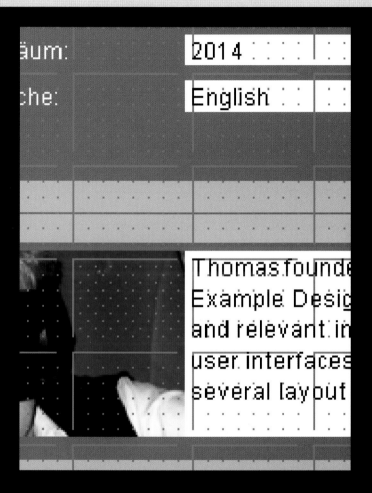

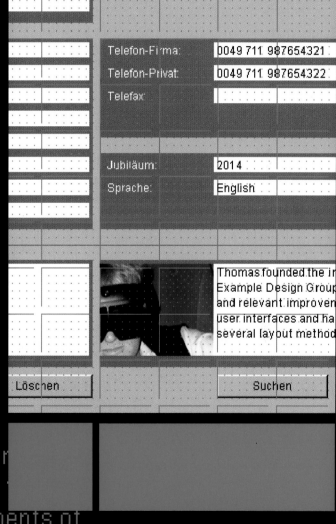

This example with inserted text elements shows how typeface sizes and line spacing can be linked to a sub-matrix – the basic principle behind layout grids in print media. This conformation can be beneficial above all where the precise positioning of text elements is concerned; for example in digital forms. The text elements

The units help to determine constant axes and positions within the layout area. These then serve the systematic structuring of the layout – although this is not always compulsory, but can be very useful – particularly with modular applications. A system of units is much more flexible for design purposes than determining

Layout grids – modularity and more

System, system, system – this could be the motto of the layout grid and this is certainly its particular strength. Yet the systematic structure of a modular interface is only one side of the coin. The other may be seen, at the very latest, when a layout concept is to be used across several different applications and media. One important area here is, for example, a corporate design for an institution, which is to be used in different media. This covers websites, Intranet applications, databases, CD-ROMs or computer-based training programs, all types of printed matter and more besides.

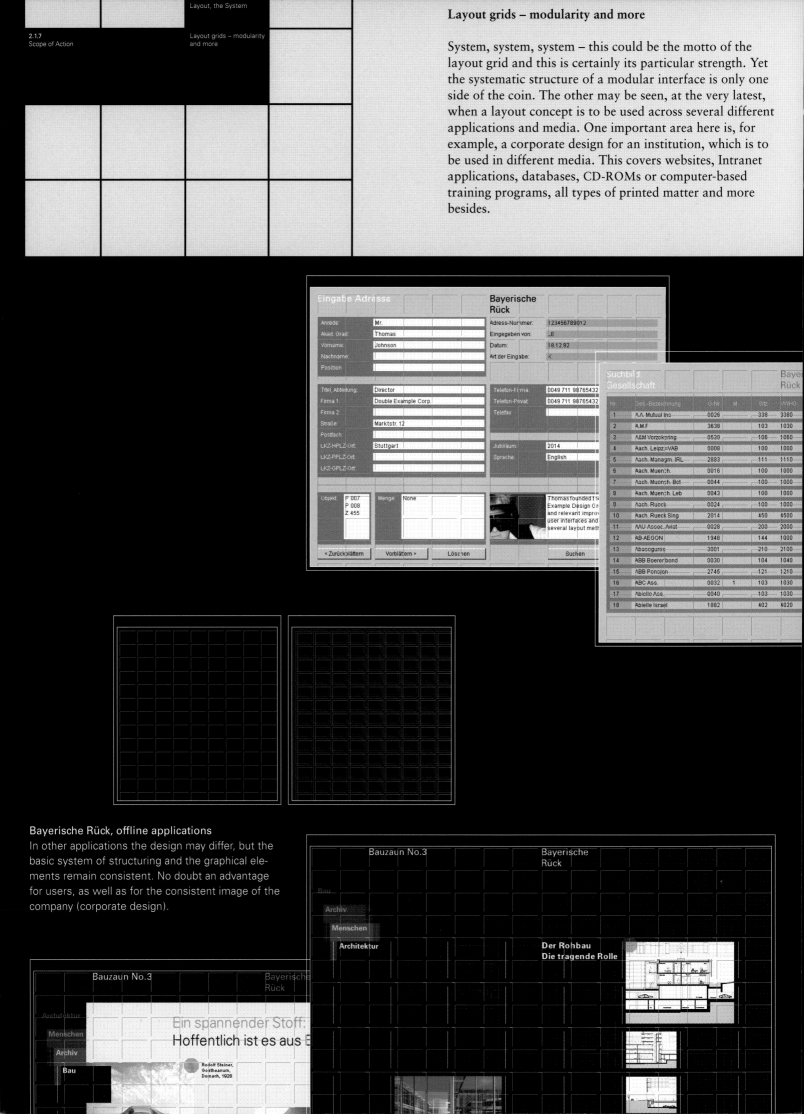

Bayerische Rück, offline applications

In other applications the design may differ, but the basic system of structuring and the graphical elements remain consistent. No doubt an advantage for users, as well as for the consistent image of the company (corporate design).

Ideally, there should at least be uniform design principles behind the digital applications, but it is even better if there are cross-media guidelines for the classical media, too. In terms of usability aspects, consistency is also a key requirement. For wherever there is much use of digital media, a consistent interface structure helps users with its orientation and use. This does not mean that digital layouts are all designed consistently the same. A few basic rules on the size and positioning often suffice to lend different applications a familiar "look and feel".

Bayerische Rück, administrative software
The layout grid facilitates the structure of the mainly modular interface. Yet not just the structure of the elements...
...but also the format of the window sizes are derived from the layout grid.

Bayerische Rück, website...
Uniform size systems based on a layout grid also allow for the use of photographs and illustrations across different media.
...and print
The same basic grid was used for print production as for digital media, considerably simplifying the exchange of graphical elements, or even allowing for automated document production. >2.2

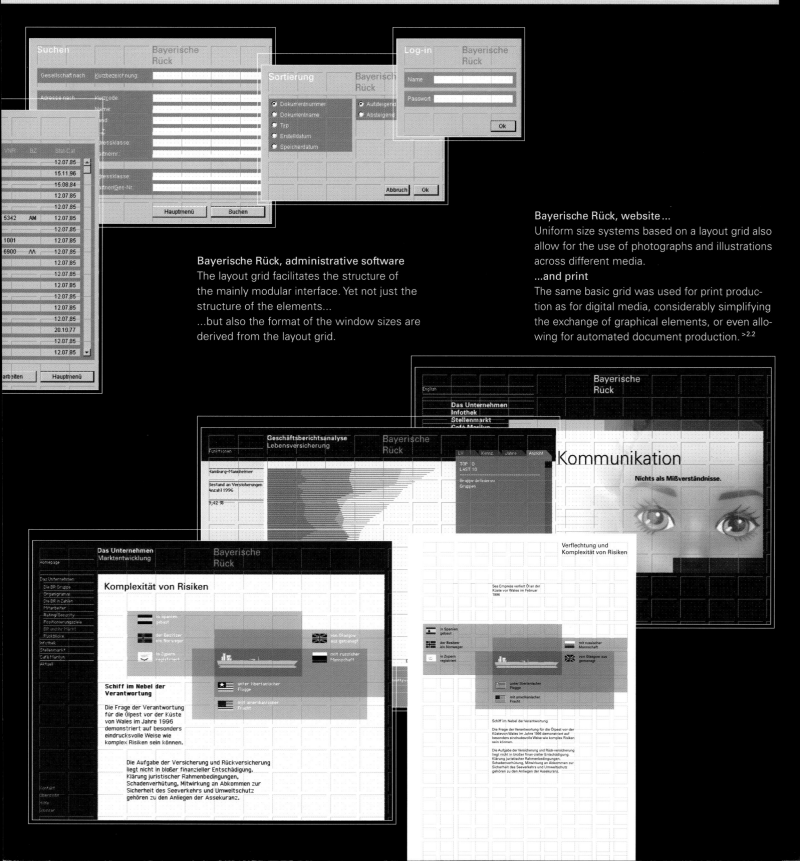

2.2.0

"Nowadays, order is usually found where there is nothing. It is in short supply."
Berthold Brecht

Topology

The term topology describes the structuring by area of the different components found in a digital layout. Descriptive elements – such as the title, as well as interactive elements – such as navigation, and contents – such as text and images, are the most important basic components of a topology. These are each assigned their own area within the layout, the position and size of which is determined over several pages, according to a uniform system. These settings are of decisive importance to the consistent appearance of a digital application, since they readily identify an application, help in differentiating between information and interactive elements and allow for fast orientation.

Standard elements, standard topology – an overview

Many websites base their topological structure on widely used standards – whether in the determination of their basic components or even their positioning within the layout area. In this example, the static interactive elements (dark blue) are found along the top edge and the dynamic navigational elements (blue) along the left edge of the layout. The owner's trademark (red) and the title (orange) are also in the upper part, ensuring that the page can still be identified when using small browser windows. The actual contents (yellow) take up the largest part in the middle, although this can be adjusted to the right by altering the size of the window.

At the bottom is the footer (green), which often contains the legal or general notes on the information available. Many topologies are structured in this or a similar way, almost lending this the quality of a standard and making it very popular – at least in terms of usability. However, this standard topology clearly shows that it is composed of static and dynamic elements. In particular, the areas for the header, navigation and contents continuously change in dimensions and size, while other elements remain unaltered. These dynamics need to be considered when planning a topology system, using correspondingly flexible areas.

A good topology fulfils these tasks in a readily identifiable manner, without becoming too restrictive. A well thought-out concept and a strong idea may be more decisive than a pedantic adherence to measurements. Many topologies in digital applications are based on conventional forms, which have become established along with developments in digital media. No doubt, this has some usability advantages, yet also easily creates a uniform layout appearance: header on top, navigation on the left, contents in the middle.

Anyone wanting to avoid this should risk breaking free of conventional patterns and ensure user-friendliness by other means: a logical concept, which is well thought-out and checked against any possible different application types within the site architecture. Even if the ordering and structure of the layouts and the development of a topology may at first appear to be purely theoretical, they cannot always be solved by abstract means. They are part of the layout process and should be structured according to the contents and the visual language.

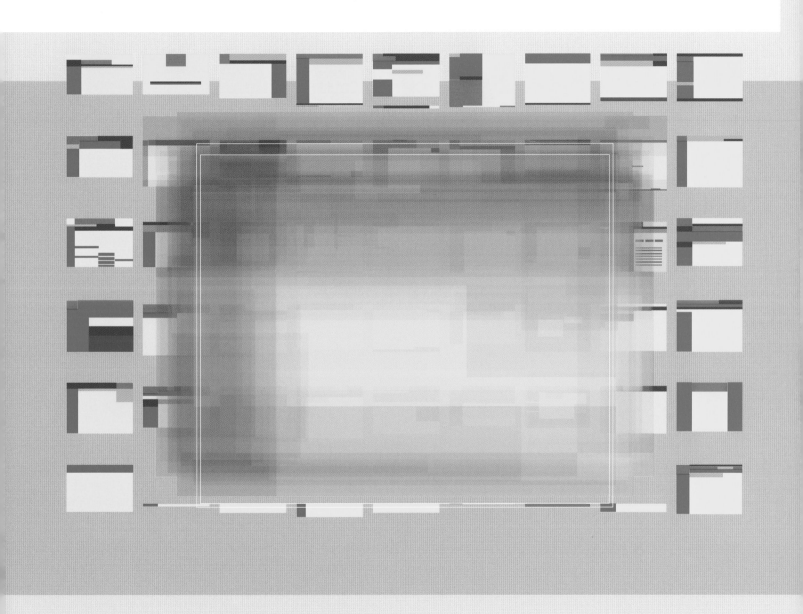

Repetition of the background image
An image which we are now used to – elements taken from 50 website topologies superimposed on one another – reveals a picture of a completely average topology. It is a fact that a large number of digital layouts rely on the features of a standard topology, as seen on the left-hand page. Familiarity may simplify things in terms of usability – although it may also hinder the development of a unique layout appearance.

The contents of a website, as well as those of any other digital application, are structured as a system of rubrics and hierarchically distributed documents. With a website, we are familiar with the example of the highest level being the "home page" together with subordinate areas for different types of content. The site architecture, that is to say the way in which these areas are structured, determines various concepts of the page layout. Pages concentrating on conveying text and images, for example, allow a different structure to those displaying forms for entering data or supporting business processes.

Diagram horizontal site:
Exemplary display of a horizontally-structured site architecture. Here, a large number of secondary pages and areas can be selected on one level. This requires a more complex organisation of the navigation (shown here as a blue sector), which has a direct effect on the structuring of the layout. The areas for the navigational elements need more space here. On the other hand, the desired contents may be reached with fewer mouse clicks, since more direct selections are on offer and the smaller number of levels requires fewer selection procedures.

A system of topologies forms the basis for structuring a layout: the division of a layout into areas reserved for particular components and functions, such as labels, or contents. Within a site architecture there is always a set of different topologies conforming to the particular characteristics of the components making up the contents. To design a digital application so that users can understand it, it helps if the work on the layouts is matched to the particular features of a site architecture – ensuring that there are no logical gaps within the topologies. The visualisation of the site architecture by way of an overview, or site map, is indispensable for this conceptual stage in the work on a layout.

This is the only way to create an overview, show the components with their interrelations and form the basis for the exemplary development of the layouts for individual page types. A site map shows where certain layout types are necessary, because in particular many or few navigation points need to be incorporated, or because the titles are important yet expendable, or because input data forms are designed differently to text pages – to name but a few examples.

Diagram vertical site:
With a vertical site architecture, the contents are divided up over more and deeper levels. Thus the pages contain fewer navigational elements, even though the user has to make more selections to reach particular information. Thanks to this site architecture, the layouts often appear simpler and the focus tends to be more on the content areas (shown in yellow here) – which has direct consequences for the development of the topology concept.

Layout, the System

2.2.2
Structure and
Organisation

Topology – the outside
view

Topology – the outside view

Ideally, the structure of a topology will first take into consideration the contextual and formal characteristics that lend it an appearance in line with the aim of the medium in question. Taking possible technical restrictions into account is also of importance, yet should not necessarily be orientated towards the most exceptional case thinkable. Worrying about the lowest monitor resolution or the smallest browser window has often killed off a good idea at the embryonic stage, without this being absolutely necessary at this early point in time.

Formal requirement
www.nytimes.com
Recognisability. "The New York Times" retains its honourable and trusted appearance even on the Internet. The website topology mainly corresponds to the print edition we know from the newspaper kiosk. Here, too, the masthead is readily identifiable at the top of the page.

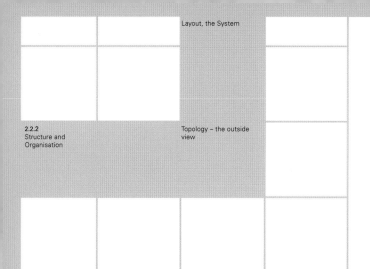

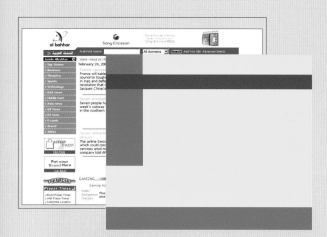

Reading directions
www.albahhar.com
Reading from left to right or from right to left. Directions in reading can affect the topological order in localised applications – even if they contain identical content.

Reading habits
www.oebb.at
Reading timetables is standardised: chronologically from top to bottom and from left to right. The Austrian Railway's online travel information retains the topological structuring of the "real", printed timetable.

Contextual or even stylistic rules, on the other hand, may be of great fundamental importance to the topology concept and usually outlast the constant changes in technology. The demands are as varied as their areas of application. A website for image purposes will be more orientated towards representative guidelines than a university's digital lecture list, while the online version of a well-established magazine will apply different requirements to the topology of the layout than a newly founded online shop. Formal requirements from other media sectors can also be important deciders for the orientation of a topological design. The recognisable style of a daily newspaper or a train timetable on the Web are examples of "visual experiences" that may be incorporated into the structure of a layout.

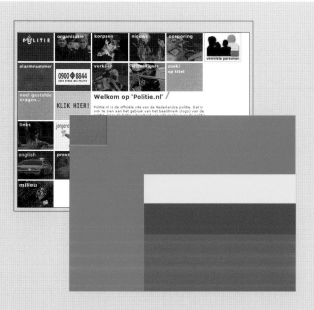
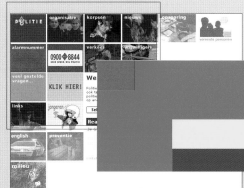

www.politie.nl
Technical requirements may be based on a certain layout topology: for example, ensuring a site is still identifiable even with the smallest of window sizes. Yet care is necessary, as the lowest common denominator often allows the smallest amount of freedom.

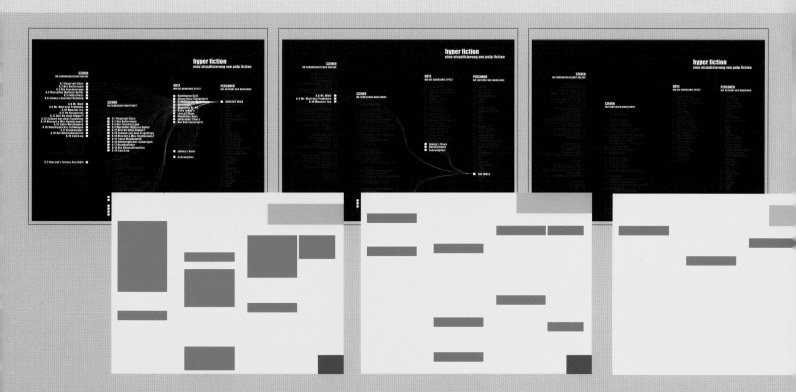

Ordering structures may be derived from contextual structures. What is really exciting is when they can be structured according to the most varied criteria.

Sascha Kempe, a student at the International School of Design in Cologne, demonstrates this in his project "HYPER FICTION", a visual and interactive illustration of the plot of "Pulp Fiction".

The contents become the navigational structure as the chronological narrative level is broken down and simultaneously becomes the interface – seen here in the contents overview. In this way the normal elements found in an ordering structure can be dissolved.

Topology – the inside view

As soon as a digital application is divided up over several screen pages, the structural characteristics of a topology aid the consistent structure of the various types of page. Here, flexibility is the key: the headers may be of different sizes, navigational elements may change in terms of scope, contents may alter their form. The concept of a topology is thus never restricted to just one page type, but is always tested with different application examples. The same applies to the addition and removal of whole parts of a topology, since the characteristic appearance of the layout should remain unaltered.

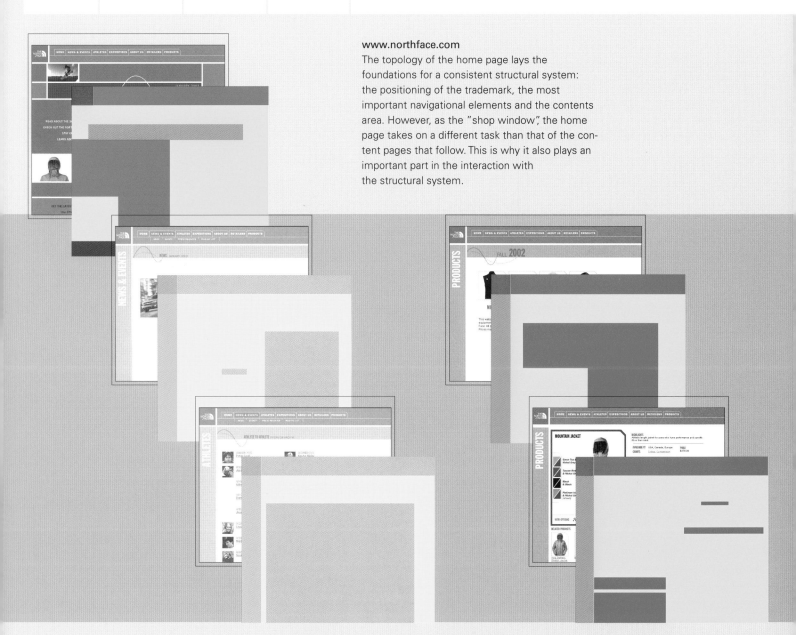

www.northface.com
The topology of the home page lays the foundations for a consistent structural system: the positioning of the trademark, the most important navigational elements and the contents area. However, as the "shop window", the home page takes on a different task than that of the content pages that follow. This is why it also plays an important part in the interaction with the structural system.

The products are presented in detail on a supplementary level or texts are displayed. These appear in additional windows, assigned to the main window. The context allows for most of the single components of the topology to be dispensed with – even the size of the window varies. This is not a problem as long as the functional principle behind the site is guaranteed by a uniform structural system in the layout concept.

From left to right and from top to bottom are the important principles for a hierarchic structuring of a digital layout – but not the only ones. The positioning ratios are completely flexible, if they are correspondingly highlighted or softened by way of their size or brightness, for example. Thus, a topology can also be turned upside down, as long as it continues to provide a clear, hierarchical structural principle. Even the positions of the individual basic components of a topology may vary from one page type to the next or simply be made available according to the relevant context.

The structure of a topology within a system is thus not slavishly tied to a rigid ordering, but is the result of a logical and unmistakable concept.

These contents pages are all structured in much the same way; merely the navigational elements within the contents area vary. A consistent system awaits the user on these levels, facilitating use and orientation.

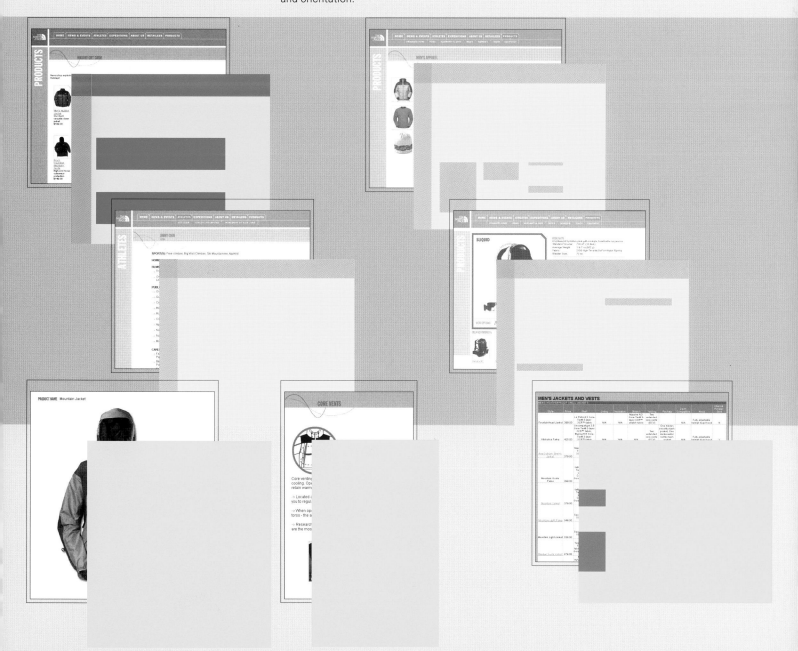

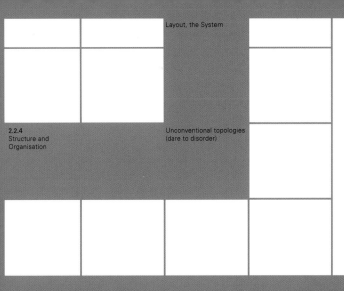

Unconventional topologies (dare to disorder)

Topological rules and their repetition are not the only factors that turn a layout into a comprehensible system. The principle behind a layout may be understood even though the rules of the topology are constantly changed and repetitions hardly ever occur. Such "unconventional" topologies allow the meaning and purpose of the individual layout components to result from the relevant context. Depending on the surroundings, for instance, they take on an identifying, controlling or informative function. In such cases, the layout is usually structured page by page and corresponds to the individual context.

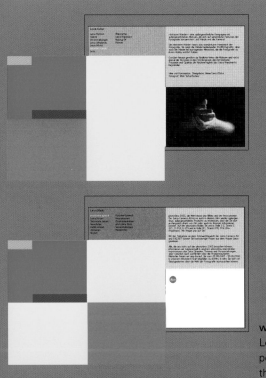

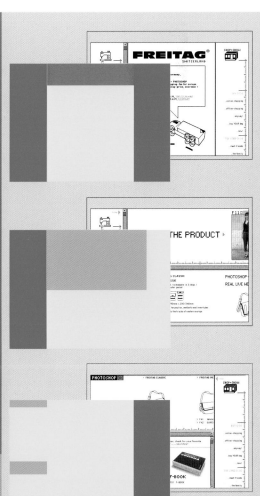

www.leica.com
Looks consistent and orderly, but it isn't: the positions of the logo and contents area alter within the rectangular page divisions. The areas for the functional elements and labels remain constant, however. This results in a clearly structured and yet dynamic image.

www.bang-olufsen.com
This website is clearly orientated along the lines of a clear formal language, which we know from the products themselves – without being limited to a schematic structure.

www.freitag.ch
The only thing here that appears to be fixed is the division into three columns. Otherwise the different elements alter their position and function at least as often as they appear. A concept whose main feature is openness.

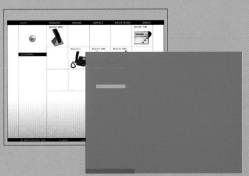

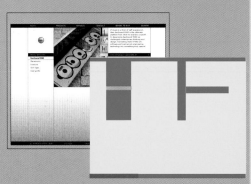

Automatic page generation and standardised maintenance is hardly possible if at all – and usually not considered, since its main purpose is to evoke as far as possible the user's own and personal experiences.

Is this allowed? Yes, indeed it should be encouraged. Because breaking free of conventional standards makes the world of digital media more exciting and varied. The desire for "low-maintenance" digital documents – structured as far as possible according to a standardised pattern and readily accessible to everybody – is an understandable concern, but one which should never lead to the senseless production of media.

Users value content on offer that is available to them in an attractive and inspirational manner, and whose structural system is not overpowering. Thus the key is to retain the balance: a conscious break with convention may refreshingly enliven an otherwise sensibly standardised system.

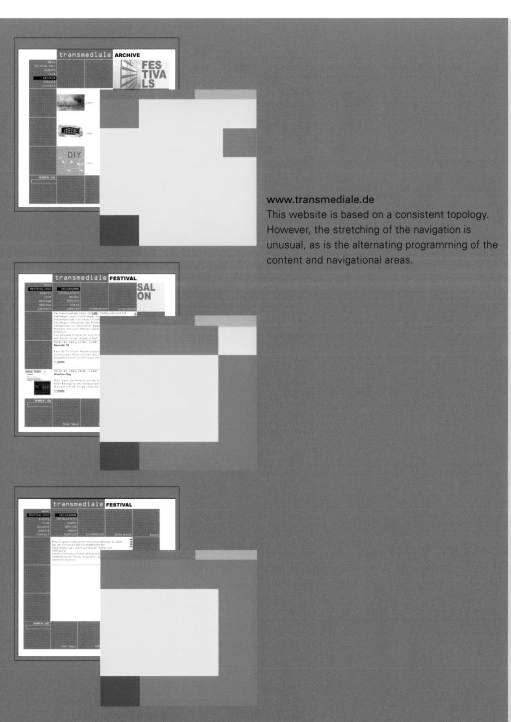

www.transmediale.de
This website is based on a consistent topology. However, the stretching of the navigation is unusual, as is the alternating programming of the content and navigational areas.

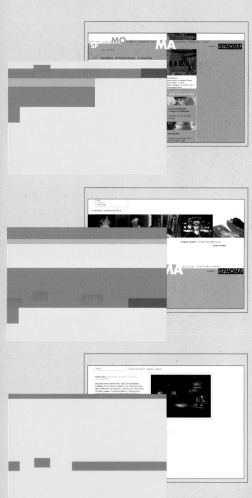

www.sfmoma.org
Depending on the contents and subject, all the components vary here and are constantly being recombined in new ways.

Structure, contents and organisation

Dynamic media with comprehensive contents are often generated from databases. Here, the contents are first stored in a database in a format independent of the layout. It is only by linking them to format templates, such as with the extensible document mark-up language (XML), that an electronic document is created. This separation of contents and form has two main advantages: firstly, the contents – mainly text and images – can be processed dynamically and irrespective of their later use, and, secondly, one and the same contents can be used for different templates and media.

**Contents and layout –
a visual summary**

**1. Database query with a
PDA browser.**
The computer and browser data are sent simultaneously to the information provider's server.

2.1 The desired information is retrieved from the database where it is stored as unformatted data – i.e. without a layout.

2.2 At the same time, the templates with the relevant topological structure are prepared, corresponding to the data specific to the device. The components and structuring of the topology is optimised for the relevant media, such as portrait mode, simplified navigation, and a limited contents area.

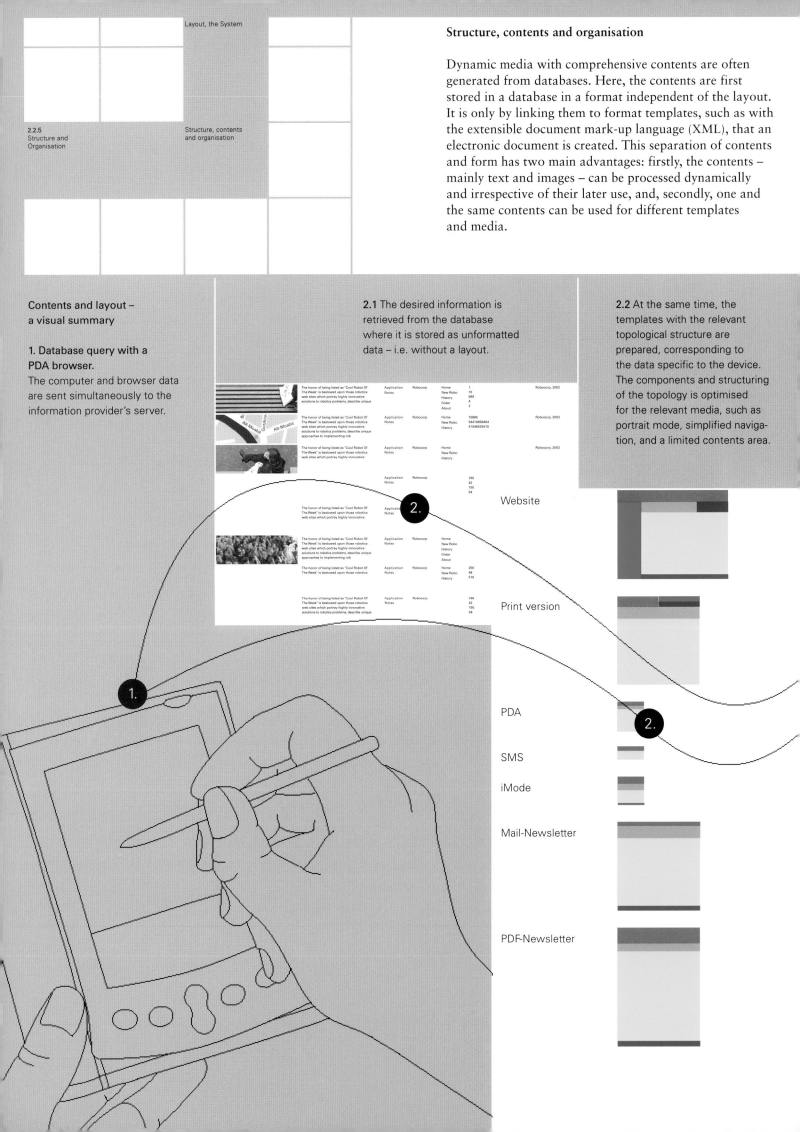

Website

Print version

PDA

SMS

iMode

Mail-Newsletter

PDF-Newsletter

However, such systems presume that the design of the templates is very highly standardised and so flexible that they can adopt different amounts of contents. Topologies play a decisive role in this system as they form the basis for a modular structuring of standardised templates and provide a starting point for the interaction between static and dynamic layout components. This allows the same contents to be presented in such media as Websites, printed matter or mobile systems, while the concept of topology ensures recognisability and comprehension across a range of media.

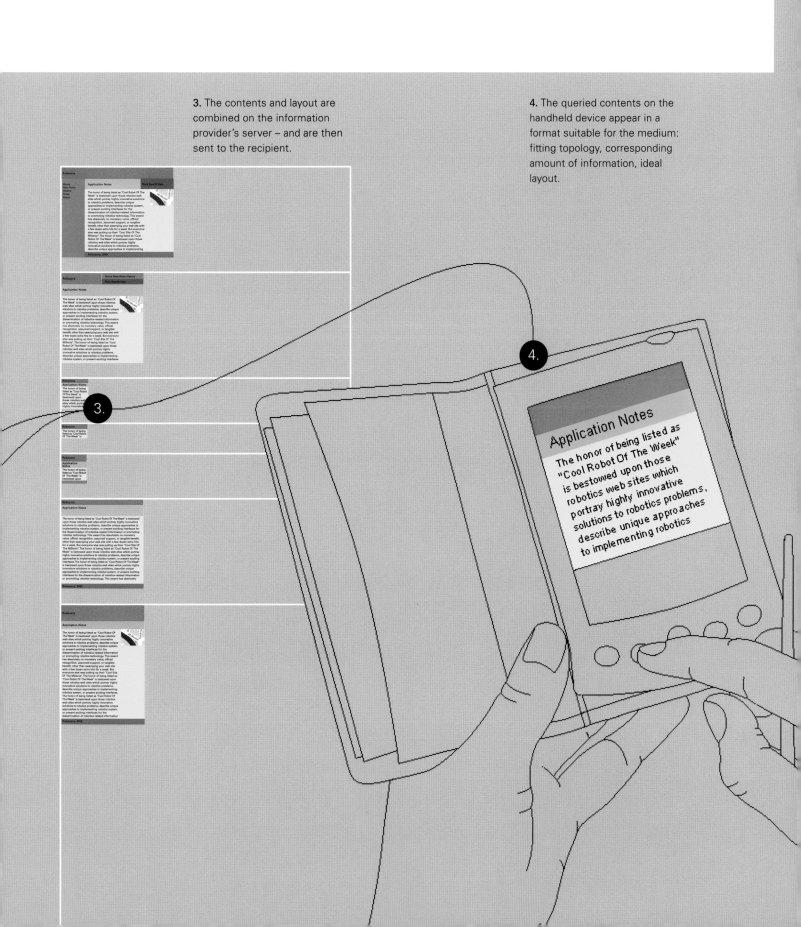

3. The contents and layout are combined on the information provider's server – and are then sent to the recipient.

4. The queried contents on the handheld device appear in a format suitable for the medium: fitting topology, corresponding amount of information, ideal layout.

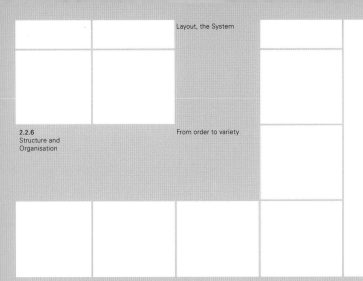

From order to variety

Ordered systems often create the impression of a lack of spontaneity and flexibility – yet they may actually contribute to this. It is only with a structured preparation of topological systems that a varied use of the same information is possible in different media, for example. The printed daily newspaper, which may exist mainly in a database, where it is updated and finally presented to the individual readers in their preferred media, is a small part of a wide spectrum of the most varied types of publication. In such cases, the layout design becomes a fine balancing of technical and graphical demands – aimed at creating an unmistakable and useful product, which gains in personality by way of the design.

Website

Print version

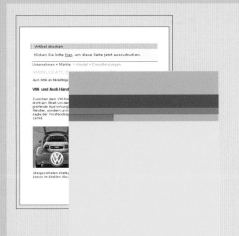

PDA

SMS

Mail-Newsletter

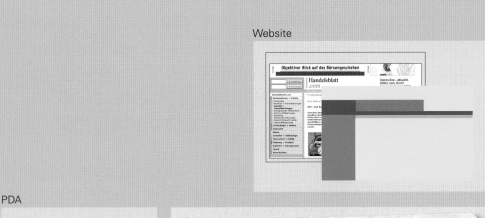

PDF-Newsletter

Most readers know the "Handelsblatt" in its printed form as a newspaper. Yet database-supported "content management" and electronic media make the contents available in other forms and media – and so maybe influence the typical image inside the readers' heads.
But what remains of the constant features?

The uniformity of topological systems naturally provides great potential for rationalisation. A whole world of brands, contents and media may be organised on the basis of a database and a set of layout templates with a well thought-out topological system. Websites are generated almost completely automatically on this principle and attain a size that could only be processed and maintained manually with great difficulty. Alterations to the image are made in a central format library, composed, in turn, of smaller, modular units, and whose elements are connected in a sensible way by a topological system.

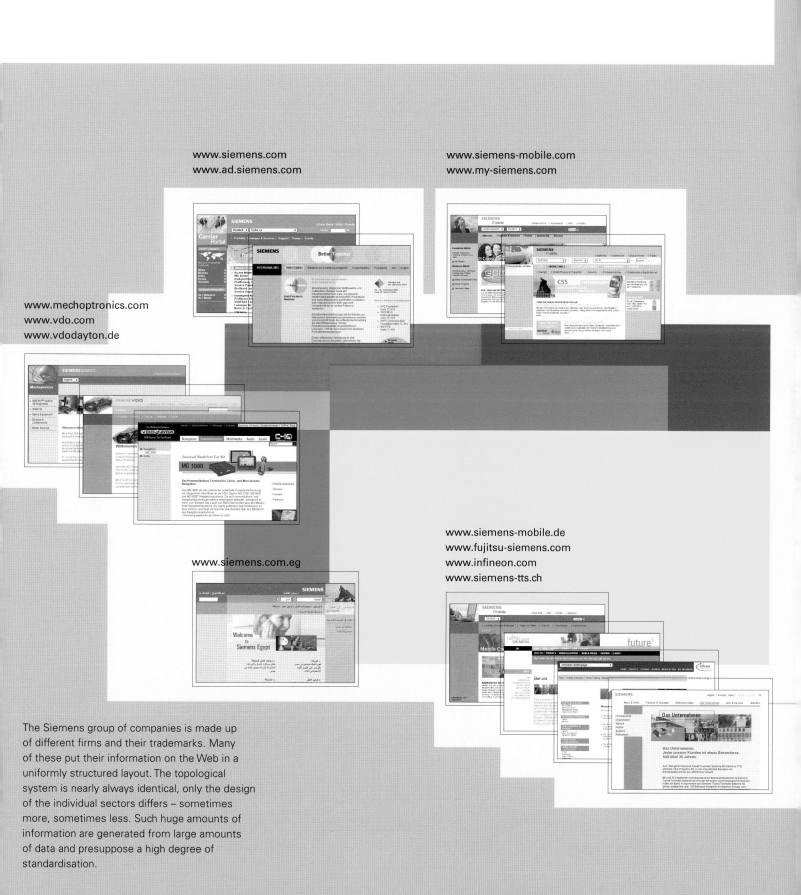

www.siemens.com
www.ad.siemens.com

www.siemens-mobile.com
www.my-siemens.com

www.mechoptronics.com
www.vdo.com
www.vdodayton.de

www.siemens-mobile.de
www.fujitsu-siemens.com
www.infineon.com
www.siemens-tts.ch

www.siemens.com.eg

The Siemens group of companies is made up of different firms and their trademarks. Many of these put their information on the Web in a uniformly structured layout. The topological system is nearly always identical, only the design of the individual sectors differs – sometimes more, sometimes less. Such huge amounts of information are generated from large amounts of data and presuppose a high degree of standardisation.

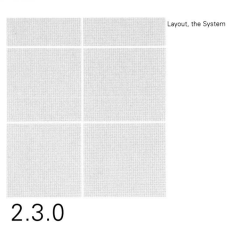

2.3.0

Collaboration

Neue Gestaltung

Branding Integration Network
Digital application to develop the corporate design
for the HypoVereinsbank

kognito

Digital media style guides for
the Bankgesellschaft Berlin

A layout is not only responsible for the visual
identity of a digital application, it also forms the
basis for collaboration within the development
process of a project – for approval with the client,
for evaluating alternative approaches and for
instructions for the technical realisation.
Cooperation always entails communication,
and here, in particular, the exchange of different
viewpoints. This is why this chapter quotes
professionals, who present their differing concepts
on the subject of dealing with the layout as the
basis for cooperation. The common denominator
is communication regarding the layout for a
financial services provider. These professionals
are two Berlin teams working at the studios
"kognito" and "Neue Gestaltung". They describe
their approaches to successful collaboration.

Layout – the communication process

As a project develops, the layout takes on various forms – from the basic design to the working model for co-operation in realising the project. This multifunctionality does not end with the development of a proposed design, but can extend much further: from the planning of a suitable presentation, right up to the creation of documentation or "blueprints" for its implementation. Depending on the demands and timing, different types of "layout communication" will be necessary, tailored to short-term events or long-term uses.

The development stages
of a project:

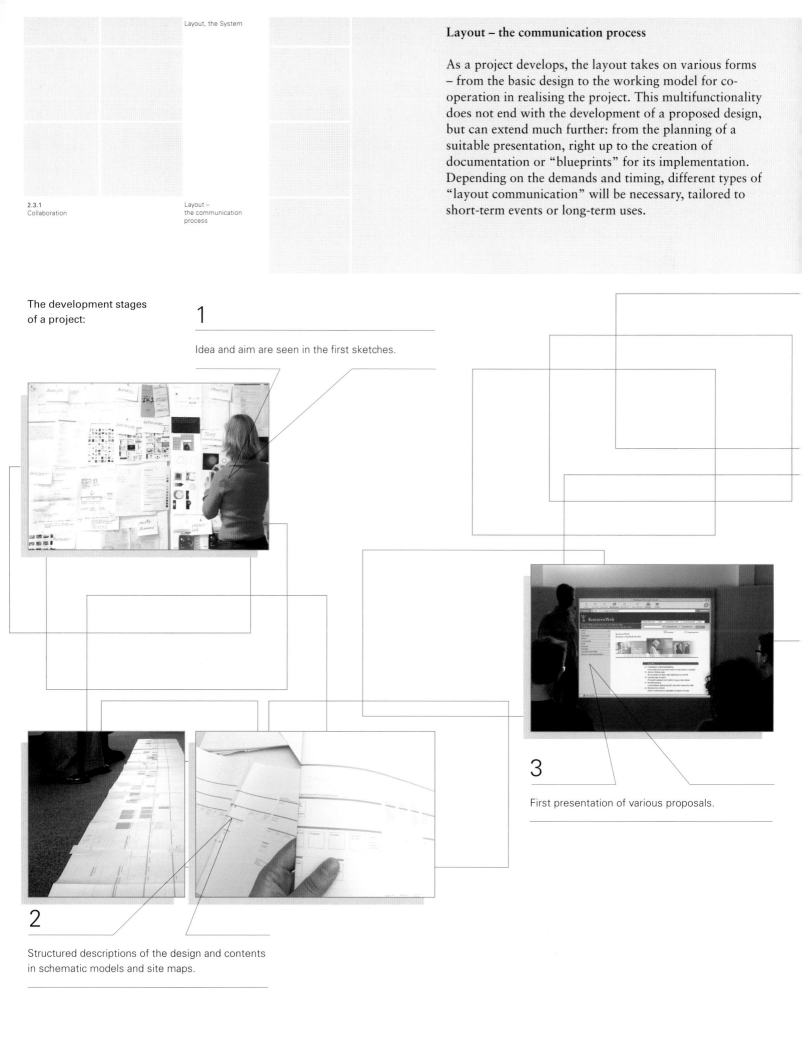

1

Idea and aim are seen in the first sketches.

2

Structured descriptions of the design and contents
in schematic models and site maps.

3

First presentation of various proposals.

One short-term example is the preparation of a layout
for a presentation in front of the client, where the focus is
more on designing the appearance and the communication
requirements of a layout. Long-term projects, on the
other hand, are documents or style guides demanding a
comprehensive description of the structure and detailed
measurements down to the last pixel within the layout.

Thus, the layout is not simply developed as an independent
design, but also a reference and description of itself,
leading in digital media to a unique subject becoming
a manifold reproducible image.

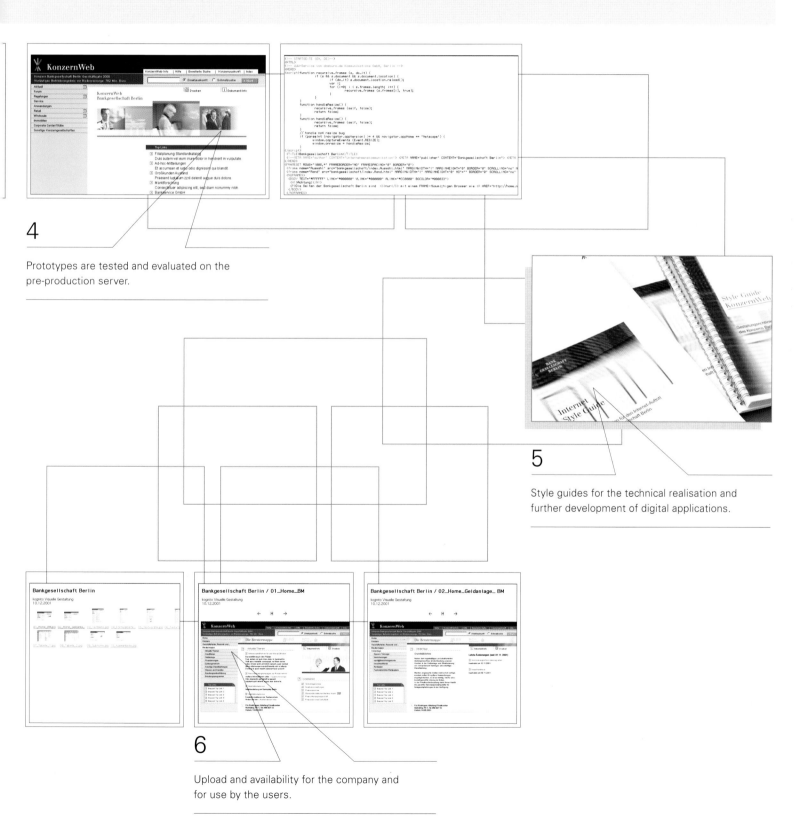

4

Prototypes are tested and evaluated on the
pre-production server.

5

Style guides for the technical realisation and
further development of digital applications.

6

Upload and availability for the company and
for use by the users.

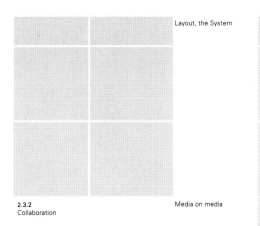

Media on media

Media on media

Layout communication means distributing different information to numerous recipients, requiring the use of different media. Often it is a question of which layout is to be used when. How can the layouts be modified or reconstructed? What functional characteristics need to be considered? In terms of design, layout communication means an unmistakable differentiation in the visual preparation: what is a component of the layout and what serves to describe and convey it? At the same time, the technical question needs to be answered: can a website even be suitably documented on another website? Is the printed form suitable as a means of documentation with regard to the rapid and repeated revision cycles?

Communication types

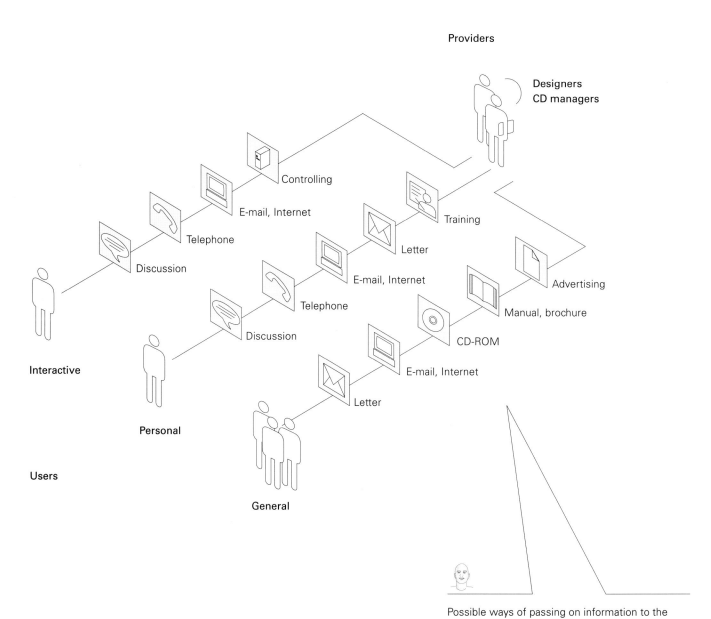

Possible ways of passing on information to the user before, during and after the layout process.

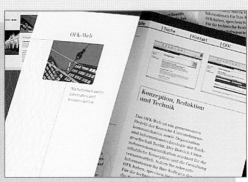

Cross-media communication: announcements and introductions help in informing large target groups and arouse curiosity across several platforms. Pictures of the layout represent the application.

Documentation and instructions allow the coordination of different specialists and the decentralised organisation of expansion and maintenance.

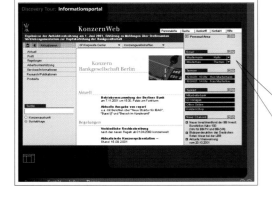

Training systems serve to introduce and set the mood for the media – using courses and training with a case study. The layout is used as the basis for the didactic process.

Cooperation interfaces – style guides

For designers, a layout is the most obvious thing in the world – for many others involved in the project it is the part of their work that needs explaining the most. Developing layouts and design systems in design manuals or style guides fills this gap. This documentation is an important working basis for the technical realisation and later maintenance of communication media – also with the aim of being able to operate without the need for an intensive supervision by the designers.
A good style guide may be a comprehensive document or program, based on an autonomous concept and tailored to the needs of the cooperation partners.

Style guide contents

1. Explanation of the aims and intentions

Corporate design digital media

1.1	Strategy and aims
1.2	Concept
1.3	Management/use/duties
1.4	Authors/responsibilities

Structure of the system

1.5	Information architecture
1.6	Site map of the contents' structure
1.7	Models/examples/detailed solutions

Contents structure

1.8	Assigning contents to page types
1.9	Presentation of page types
1.9.1	Home page
1.9.2	Sub home page
1.9.3	Text pages

What do we need to know in order to gain as detailed an image of the layout as possible? This comprehensive list shows what has to be defined during the layout process and thus what is important for other members involved in the project.

2. Design concept

Page structure

2.1	Description of the topology
2.2	Page structure
2.3	Window types

Headers and footers

2.4	Components and their functionality
2.5	Measurements

Navigation

2.6	Components and their functionality
2.7	Labelling
2.8	Measurements

3. Example applications

Design templates/examples and measurements

3.1	Home page
3.2	Sub home page
3.3	Text pages, single-column layout
3.4	Text pages, multi-column layout
3.5	Tables
3.6	Graphics
3.7	Input masks
3.8	Lists
3.9	Site map
3.10	Contacts

Documentation and measurement of the design components

3.1	Logos
3.2	Typeface
3.3	Links
3.4	Colour palettes
3.5	Icons
3.6	Visual language
3.7	Functional elements
3.8	Teasers
3.9	Dividing/structuring elements
3.10	Coding elements

Animations

3.11	Use/formats
3.12	Formal design
3.13	Movement
3.14	Interactivity

4. Instructions on use and maintenance

Instructions

4.1	Creating graphic components
4.2	Diagram of work process

The main focus is on four subject areas: explanation of the aims and intentions of the contents, description of the design concept, example applications, and instructions on its expansion and maintenance.

Hardly any style guide is actually finished at the time of its publication, which is why a modular, expandable structuring of its contents is strongly recommended. Additions occurring, for example, in later operation and in maintaining a website, absolutely need to be incorporated into the style guide to ensure a consistent documentation. This may seem like a lot of work – and it is.

Style guides are often disregarded as "by-products", comfortably placed on the level of measured layout designs. A well-structured style guide, optimally tailored to meet the user group's needs, may well mean more work, yet a worthwhile and valuable investment for any client. Its further development is orientated towards clear guidelines and may be adopted by different partners within a foreseeable introductory period. Using this common foundation stone, those involved in the project become the project's partners.

It is important that style guides do not simply gather dust on shelves or hard disks, but are actively used in workshops or as part of a wide-ranging information campaign, for example.

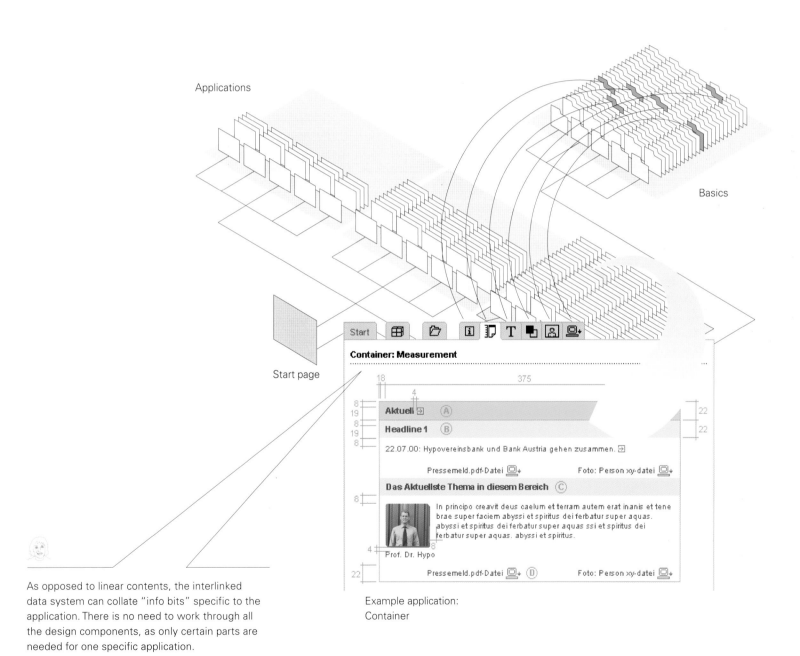

As opposed to linear contents, the interlinked data system can collate "info bits" specific to the application. There is no need to work through all the design components, as only certain parts are needed for one specific application.

Example application:
Container

The Bankgesellschaft Berlin Intranet, called
KonzernWeb, is an extremely comprehensive
and complex medium which contains several
thousand documents. Decentralised technical
and textual maintenance is often the only way of
ensuring the operation of such a system. The
documentation is made available online as PDFs
or, where it makes sense, in printed form.

2.3.3
Collaboration

Examples here are included in their entirety. The
user can perceive the whole page at a glance. The
pages contain different types of windows with page
structure, frame and grid division as well as explanations of all the components. The colour coding of
the frames is consistent and facilitates recognition
of the different types of window. These are set in
a colour that is not otherwise found in the layout.

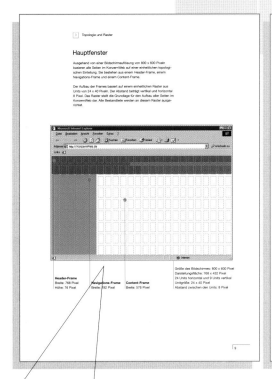

The starting parameters of screen resolution and
browser program are defined. This guarantees
a uniform base.

A printed style guide allows for a better
comparison of the example pages. Since it is
a constant reference, the style guide is always
available. There is no need to click back and forth
between the pages.

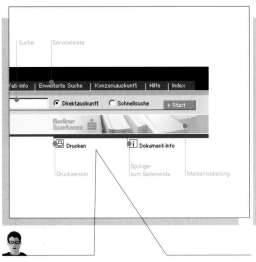

Uniform naming, so that all those involved
know what is being talked about. Nothing aids
communication as much as a uniform vocabulary.

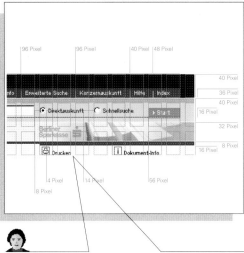

Grid systems and precise measurements, so
that there are no misunderstandings during
the technical side of the programming process.

BRAIN (Branding Integration Network) is a digital tool (brand tool) for defining the HypoVereinsbank corporate design.
The following examples show the procedure when an electronic medium is accessed.

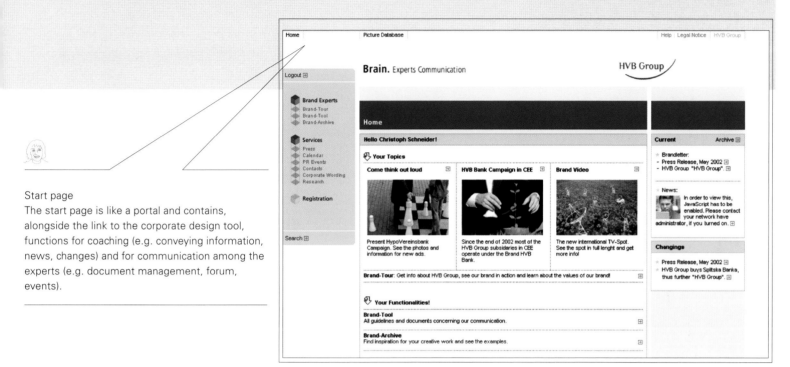

Start page
The start page is like a portal and contains, alongside the link to the corporate design tool, functions for coaching (e.g. conveying information, news, changes) and for communication among the experts (e.g. document management, forum, events).

Selected page: applications
In the first stage, the brand tool is shown for the application structure throughout the company. This includes electronic media as well as advertising, business stationery or publications.

In particular "function-heavy" pages need to be described in great detail and comprehensively, since this is where vague descriptions may lead to misunderstandings, which in turn may result in wasted time and unnecessary costs.

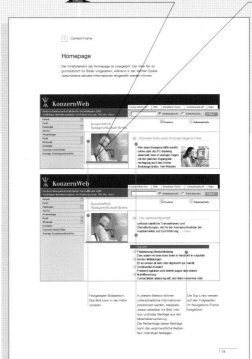

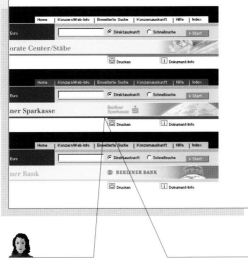

Detailed visualisations, so that difficult components and functions may be understood and reconstructed in detail.

Redundant documentation: examples, examples, examples – the more detailed, the better. Many new applications are usually just slight variations on existing ones.

To design page descriptions in a comprehensible manner, the explanations and measurements are divided up over consecutive pages. First the general page functions are described, then the measurements down to the last pixel.

Measurements should be designed uniformly throughout the whole style guide: same colour, font, type size, line type, as well as the format and position in relation to the example, all help the user. Layout components need to be enlarged, so that the details may be implemented.

Pages with a collection of individual layout elements provide readers with an overview of the different types and their applications. This also facilitates the creation of new components, since further elements can be developed in the same style.

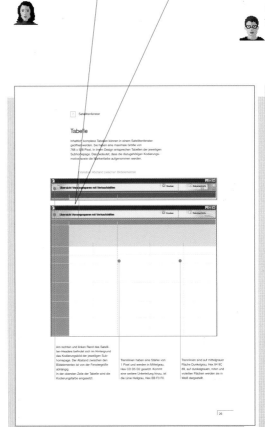

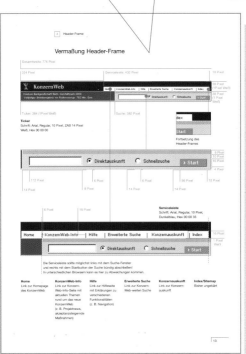

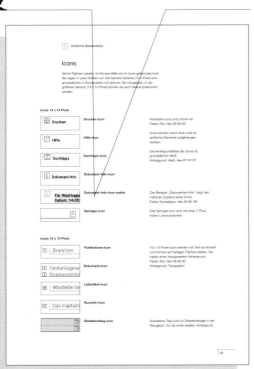

Selected page: Electronic media:
This page contains an overview of the structure
of the application group electronic media.
The desired application may be selected here.

Selected subpage: Here there follows a list of the
components belonging to the selected application,
e.g. for a subpage the measurements for the
whole page, top navigation, containers, etc.

The "tabs"
The corporate design (CD) was split into its
basic elements, saved as modular pieces and
filed under application-specific tabs, like in a card-
index system. Tabs contain the information on
measurements, logos, fonts, colours, processing,
photo and illustration languages, as well as
structuring principles.

Measurement
The "tabs" contain the requirements for the page
components with detailed measurements and
explanatory text. Information and coaching is needed prior to downloading the instruments, so as to
minimise their wrong use.

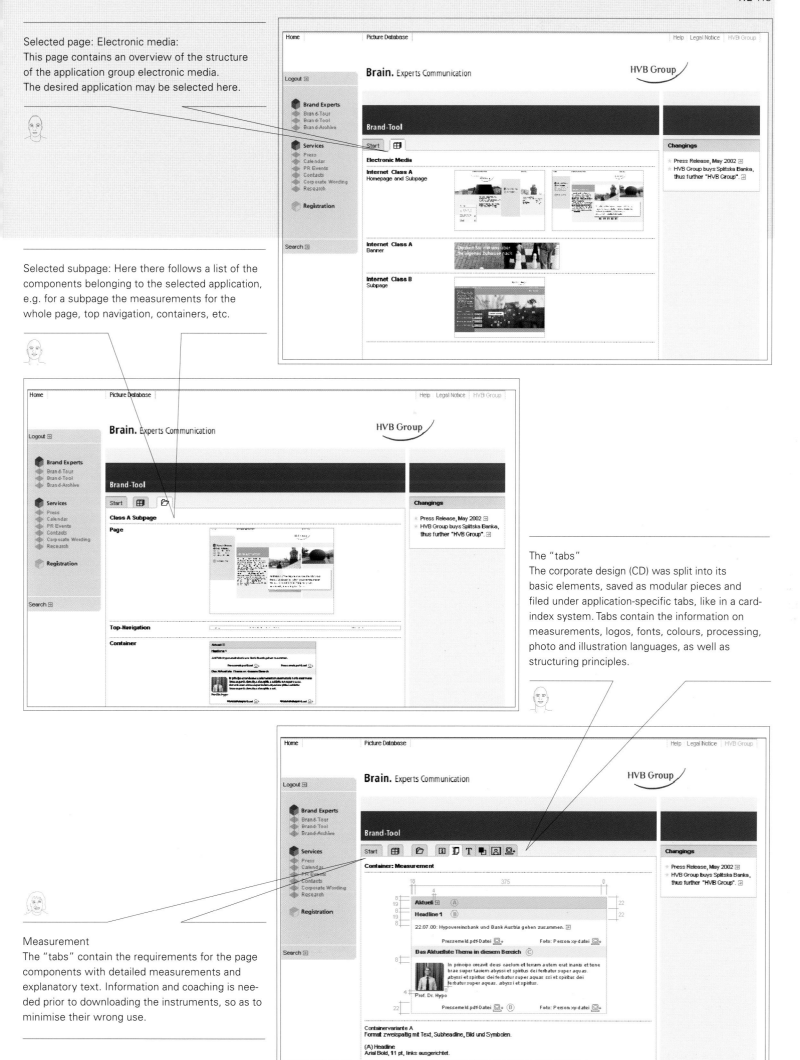

Digital kits

All permanent and recurring layout components can be made available in a building block system for use as digital working materials. And here, too, compliance with pre-defined conventions in naming and structuring can be of great help.
Example files need to be absolutely reliable, as they are almost certain to be copied many times and distributed digitally. It is best to do away with cryptic labels and to ensure that graphic components structured in layers have a consecutive labelling. The distribution, whether via data medium or online, needs to be clearly pre-defined for the group of recipients.

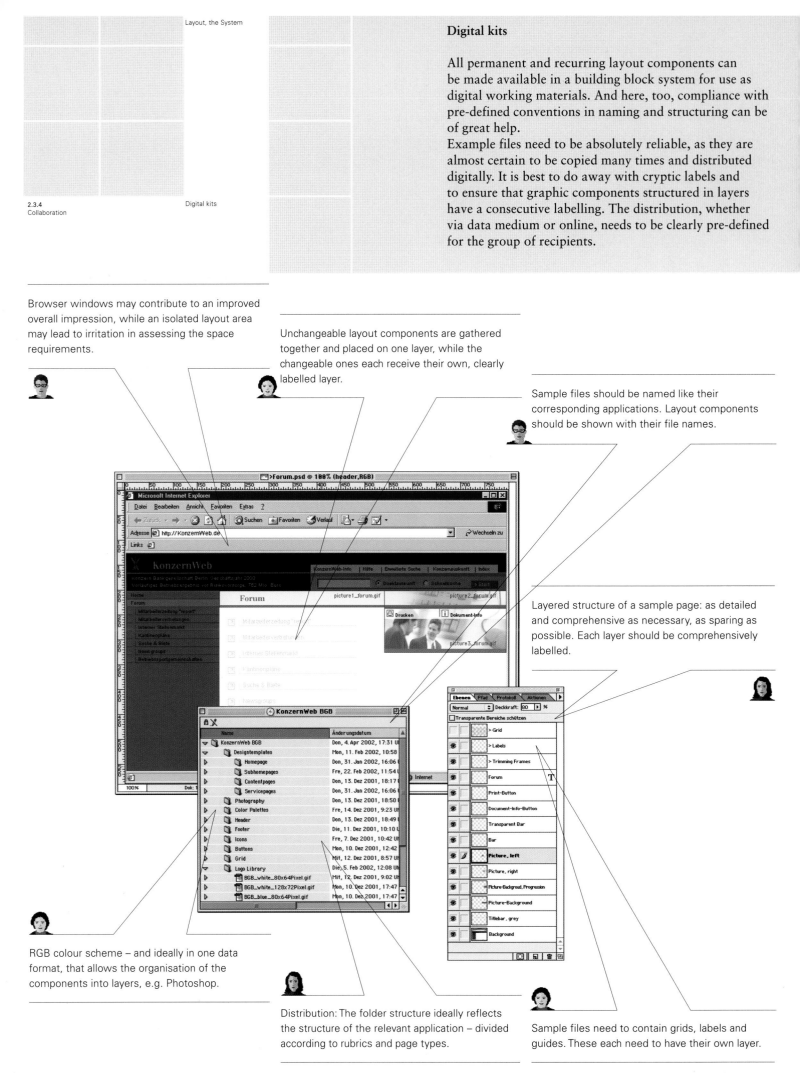

Browser windows may contribute to an improved overall impression, while an isolated layout area may lead to irritation in assessing the space requirements.

Unchangeable layout components are gathered together and placed on one layer, while the changeable ones each receive their own, clearly labelled layer.

Sample files should be named like their corresponding applications. Layout components should be shown with their file names.

Layered structure of a sample page: as detailed and comprehensive as necessary, as sparing as possible. Each layer should be comprehensively labelled.

RGB colour scheme – and ideally in one data format, that allows the organisation of the components into layers, e.g. Photoshop.

Distribution: The folder structure ideally reflects the structure of the relevant application – divided according to rubrics and page types.

Sample files need to contain grids, labels and guides. These each need to have their own layer.

It is also important to clarify a number of questions. Who receives what data? How is the modification or even creation of new layouts regulated? Who authorises what? Who is responsible for quality assurance?
In most cases the client has a vested interest in seeing that the distribution and use of the data is confined to very tight circles and conforms to the approved standards. Conversely, designers often ruin their own work when they do not cooperate in making the data available – an unfortunate consequence is when the client takes over control and unprofessional modifications are made to the layout.

Download
The "Download" tab allows users to download all materials, templates and rules relevant to the project. For example, this is a pre-formatted layout file for a poster with the relevant logo and a PDF file containing all the rules and measurements.

Clarity
Since users receive their materials specific to their target group and applications, only the necessary rules and materials are provided. This helps make the rules comprehensible and reduces the source of errors. Here, intelligent filters and structures ensure a simple description of the application and a distribution of the instruments, which is both finely structured and tailored to the needs.

Double coaching
The whole equipment is maintained and represented both as an online description and as files for downloading.

Updating
Thanks to the modular structuring, only the relevant basic modules need to be altered to enable users to receive current or revised files. This ensures that only valid rules and data are used at all times.

Info agents
The coaching is extended by way of an alteration management system, which immediately informs users of changes to the corporate design definitions.

3.1.0

Mobile devices

Unlimited mobility leads to the most varying scopes of effect for the use of digital media. It is of absolutely no importance as to when or where they are used, yet the demands made of the user are particularly high: the display sizes are very limited yet must incorporate a large number of functions, such that mobile devices do not allow much scope for differentiated and refined design elements within a layout. The main criterion here is a clear and informative presentation of the contents, represented in turn by navigable structures.

Navigation systems

Look, steer, brake – the scope of effect formed by vehicle and traffic may certainly be considered a particularly stressful one. While information systems in vehicles may be linked to acoustic signals, fast legibility of the display is of decisive importance here. A link to familiar visual languages, such as traffic signs or road atlases, is certainly a great help.

Mobile phones

These "constant companions" are used everywhere and at any time. Their scopes of effect can hardly be delimited and thus demand easily and quickly comprehensible interface layouts for mobile, graphical services. Mass products, such as mobile telephones, arouse the need for a personal touch – provided by phone covers.

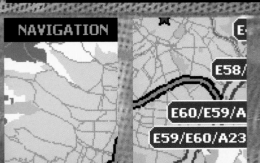

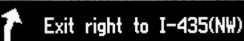

Navigation and contents very much form one unit and need to be structured so that they can simultaneously take on a controlling function, while providing information on their type and scope.

Mobile media usually belong to individuals and their owners often cultivate a close relationship with their constant companion. Often the device itself is personalised and accessorised – in complete contrast to the rather brief and sober forms of expression seen on the display. Thus it is not the display layout that can be judged for its "coolness" or conventionality, but rather the device cover.

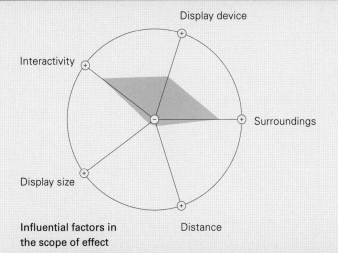

Influential factors in
the scope of effect

PDA/handhelds
These allow more complex applications in independent scopes of effect. Here, more comprehensive and more personal activities are also carried out, often necessitating a quieter corner.

What is exciting is when the mobile medium creates a direct link to its surroundings, such as in a museum. The scope of effect and layout then directly interact and should be visually adapted to one another.

Desktop systems

Concentration, controlled environment, optimised technologies – in no other scope of effect does a digital application receive so much attention as at the workplace or at home. This means that correspondingly intensive and generous use may be made of the visual design possibilities. Media at work or at home are in a personally controlled and protected sphere. The user is often more trusting and willing to experiment; personal preferences are tolerated or even remain unnoticed. This may, at most, lead to collisions of taste or semantics in the scope of effect and layout.

Those who do not own their own personal computer system often resort to publicly available offers, such as Internet cafés. Here, the public surroundings are simply blocked out of the personal perception so as to be able to concentrate on surfing, e-mails or even work.

Even the time factor hardly plays a role here, and there is also a high degree of readiness to deal with something new or surprising.

Layouts for these scopes of effect may display much detail and complex structures; the ratio between text and images to the layout area is at its most favourable and the range of possible designs the widest.

Display device

Interactivity

Surroundings

Display size

Distance

Influential factors in the scope of effect

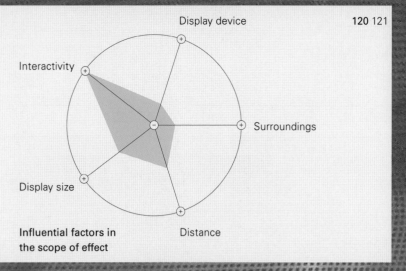

Workplace or living room – dealing intensively with digital content always requires a certain amount of concentration and peace. Once this is guaranteed, the complexity of the visual representation may be higher – if necessary: more elements, lower contrasts, smaller font sizes, etc. However, "semantic collisions" are unavoidable when personal preferences extend from the display background into the surroundings. More on this, incidentally, in Chapter 3.3.

Public terminals

Berlin. Tiergarten suburban railway station. The next train can already be seen approaching. Is there time to quickly buy a ticket now or wait until the next train comes?
A question that can easily depend on the design of the ticket-machine interface. The design of layouts for public use is rigorously orientated towards user-friendliness and efficacy. This is not just a matter of dramatic scenarios – like the time pressure described above – it is also an expectation of direct benefit, which is decisive for the quality of an application. The public scope of effect is an impersonal one and one influenced by numerous environmental factors: changing lighting conditions, restless passers-by, surprising events. This requires a high

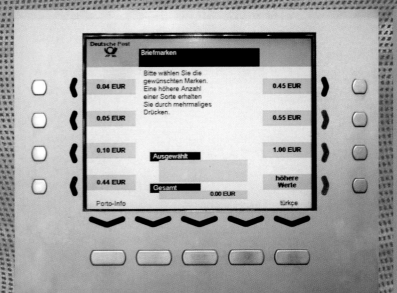

Displays in public terminals often directly interact with their immediate surroundings in that the functions of their buttons are assigned to real buttons...
Deutsche Post stamp vending machine

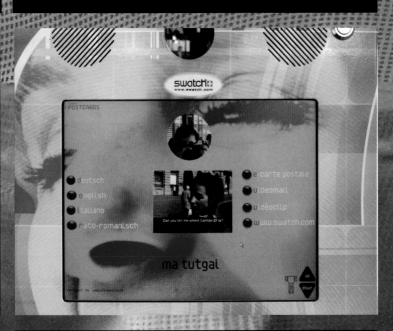

...by completing the interface, helping to compensate for gaps in comprehension and thus continuing the layout beyond virtual space into real space.
Deutsche Bahn ticket vending machine

...by simply making the user part of the application –
and thus part of the layout.
Make a wish, "SWISH" Pavilion, Expo02 Biel/Switzerland

...in that the scope of effect melts into the application and the application melts into the scope of effect. The media-independent layout, in this case an illustrative face, is intended to help suggest a unit that does not actually exist.
A Swatch info-terminal

degree of personal concentration and yet is hardly suitable for a personalised offer, with the odd exception, such as ATMs. Thus, in an almost logical counter reaction to the extremely low "tolerance threshold", use is often made of physical buffer zones: the terminals are intended to strongly focus on the display, by spatially protecting it or by adopting a direct visual connection to the interface layout. In the most unfavourable case, they even have to face up to their own interface design deficits. Designing a layout for public space means making a connotative link between the real and the virtual world. In so doing, the proportions are considerably enlarged, such that a system can be operated by a touch screen alone without any further input devices.

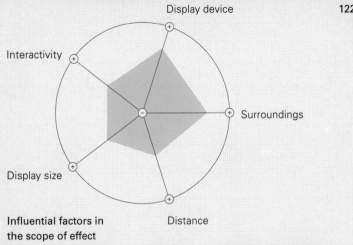

Influential factors in the scope of effect

- Display device
- Interactivity
- Surroundings
- Display size
- Distance

The scope of effect as a common space. Those who prefer a private atmosphere will only occasionally make use of public terminals. There are always hurdles to overcome: Am I doing everything right? Are my interests embarrassing? Who is looking over my shoulder?

Light blue paintwork, pink upholstery and chrome exhaust. Because reality suppresses it, sales people are not confident enough and because it is fun. Fortunately the info-configuration-terminal really exists...
Volkswagen Phaeton presentation lounge

The scope of effect as a performance, in that the display design sets a certain tone. This then attracts visitors.
Info-terminals in the "Biopolis" Pavilion, Expo02/Switzerland

The private sphere in a public space – even for surfing cyclists. A comfortable way of gaining access to the content on offer on the Internet.
e-info station in Berlin

Large-size displays and projections

It is often a strange situation for all concerned: layouts developed on the desktop are then shown to an audience. Presentations should really be designed from the audience's viewpoint. Many things could then be more easily adapted to the specific demands made by the situation. The scope of effect and presentation are closely linked, they can mutually strengthen the effect, dampen it or even negate it. Apart from the spatial influences, a further, more decisive factor stems from the unfamiliar setting: the presentation moves on and the audience needs to follow. This becomes a challenge once the contents are not linearly structured, but instead are equipped with the refinements of an interactive application. Guidelines on preparing a

Globe
Reality as a layout – here there is not so much to design, yet more to stare at. The scope of effect and media are perfectly aligned to the content. This digital globe in the Tokyo Museum for Research and Technology displays time-lapse satellite images of the Earth. A circular ramp allows the world to be circumnavigated in just a few steps, while info-terminals provide additional information.

Presentation
Projected presentations always create a "three-way relationship" between the speaker, presentation area and audience, automatically resulting in a strong spatial context. Projections often presuppose a dimming of the lighting, focusing attention on the illuminated projection area. The speaker takes control of the visual events; interaction is – at best – only possible by interruption. Layouts for such purposes need to be simple, clear, well organised and as easily understandable in their storyline as possible.

presentation often talk about "getting to the point", so as to gain – and keep – the audience's attention. This is pretty much the opposite of the case with user-controlled, interactive systems: here the user's own initiative gets to the point. Presentations, whether in the open or in a closed space, incorporate their surroundings: ideally they are based on a spatial performance and a concept that allows the scope of effect to become an integral part of the event. The site of the presentation area and the graphic design, as well as optimisation with a view to the audience's perception should follow a clear focus: fewer graphical elements, good legibility at different distances and a comprehensible structure. And, as already stated, ideally designed from the audience's viewpoint.

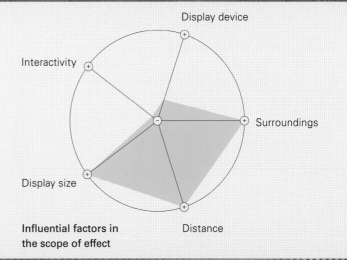

Influential factors in the scope of effect

NASA mission control
Total concentration. A number of different media are used at NASA mission control. Some of the displays are so large that all those present in the room can read them at once, whether they are standing right in front of them or in the far corner of the room. The workplace equals the scope of effect – this often means that the environmental factors need to be reduced to a minimum: in this example by dimming the lighting.

360 degrees
Scopes of effect are always places of experience. This is particularly evident where the tangible space becomes a physical experience. A 360-degree projection, which places the observer at the centre of the medium, is an impressive experience in itself. The required size of the space and the medium further enhance this impression. Sometimes even more than the actual contents of the projection.
Scene from the "Panorama" Pavilion, Expo02/Switzerland

3.2.0

Information capacity of the sensual organs

We register by far the most information visually:
In terms of the amount of information, the eyes
form the centre of human perception. Yet this
does not detract from the importance of the
other senses, such as touching or hearing.
As is so often the case, Aristotle's much-quoted
observation applies: The whole is more than
the sum of all of its parts – even if the following
chapter is mainly concerned with the visual
aspects of the digital layout.

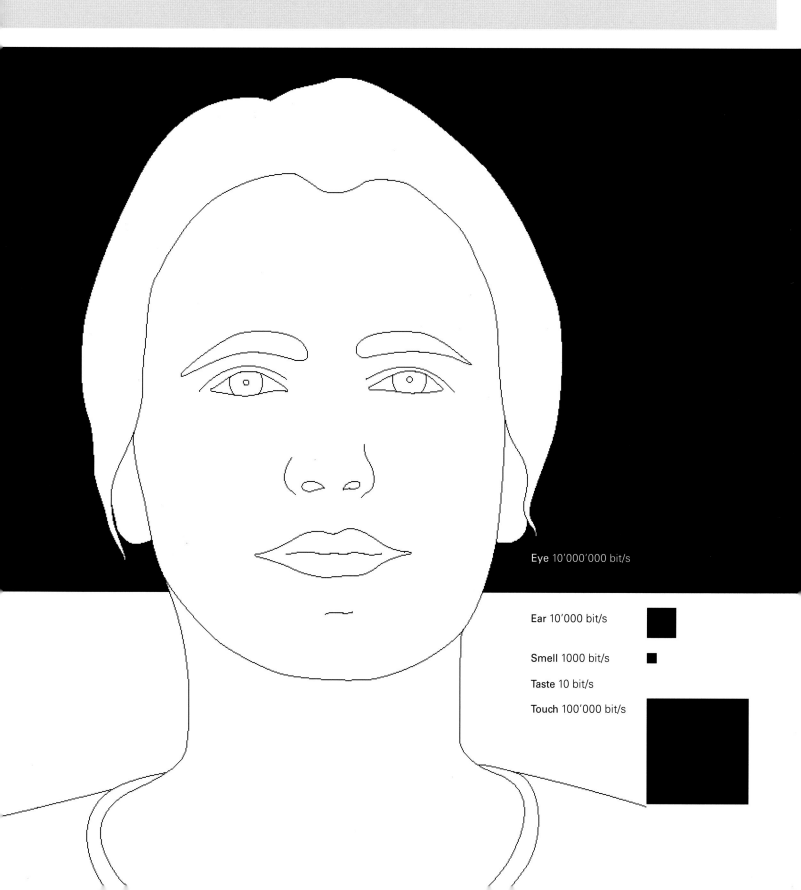

Eye 10'000'000 bit/s

Ear 10'000 bit/s

Smell 1000 bit/s

Taste 10 bit/s

Touch 100'000 bit/s

Perception – no accident

The world of digital media offers us a large number of new possibilities and impressions. Yet at least when it comes to our habits of perception, we repeatedly realise that these are still closely intertwined with the world of traditional media.

Digital media are "interest" media. That is to say that due to the interactive possibilities we often let ourselves be completely freed from our interests and only perceive those that appear to really interest us. More so than with linear media, for example, such as a film or a conventional book, maintaining interests with selectively perceived digital media represents a constant challenge.

Attention
Larger, brighter, faster, louder? Not just this. Even subtle stimuli gain our attention, by appealing to basic mental patterns, such as the orientation reflex. Of importance here is that if several stimuli are used at once, they may strengthen or neutralise each other.

Intensity
Size, brightness, speed or loudness generally focus the attention on themselves. The larger, brighter, faster or louder, the more the orientation reflex is stimulated.

Exception
Stimuli, which stand out from their surroundings, or break out of a series, are particularly noticeable.

Magic 7
The "magic 7", as it is called even by experienced cognition scientists, describes the state whereby only around 7 (+/– 2) independent units of information may be processed in our short-term memory. Whoever takes this form of simplicity into consideration when designing the layout can considerably improve the user-friendliness.

Chunking
This is the organisation of information into manageable units of perception: only the second row of numbers can be processed.

17891918194519892001

1789 1918 1945 1989 2001

Structuring of rubrics
An easily comprehensible number of rubrics simplifies orientation and allows a more spontaneous differentiation into intelligible units.

The process of perception
Perception is composed of a series of different perception events. The path from the sensual organ to the processing regions of the brain and finally the conclusion drawn is a matter of a few seconds.
The layout design can facilitate or hinder this process: comprehensible and clear types of expression accelerate the perception process, while puzzling and opaque ones complicate it.

Sensorial sensitivity
Light is absorbed and transformed into neuronal activity by the brain cells.

Perception
The representation of the perceived, the "percept", is assigned to a provisional image.

For working on the layout a whole series of different instruments is available for controlling interests; and at first it appears easy to resort to the spectacular, loud and penetrating – which unfortunately is all too often the case. Yet the spectrum of perception control has more to offer: types of differentiation, which subtly accentuate by way of the unknown or noticeably restrained and thus trigger equally attractive stimulants in the brain. The game of the unknown constantly arouses curiosity and is wonderfully suited as an alternative to the visual barrage, from which we so often seek refuge as fast as possible.

Innovation
If the classification within the perception process is hindered, because something new can not immediately be assigned, this attracts our attention.

Irritation
Deviations from known patterns also grab our attention.

Instinct
Gestures, faces or even sexual stimuli are inborn triggers that automatically gain our attention.

Navigation
A larger number of elements may be grouped together as comprehensible units by way of a hierarchy.

Structuring according to units
Even with a modular structuring of the layout, it is necessary to retain an overview; because only a limited number of modules may be quickly perceived.

Text coding
Typographic labelling, such as headlines, body copy, highlighting etc. should be used sparingly. Too much means that they cannot easily be differentiated and so hardly have any function.

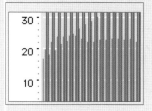

Colour coding
It is almost impossible to recall too many colour codes, especially on the computer screen, with its varying sizes and qualities of representation. Thus it is strongly recommended that the "magic 7" is adhered to here.

Classification
The temporary image is compared to known patterns, assigned and understood.

The first impression
Processing the information into the "first impression": for example, agreeable or unpleasant, interesting or boring.

Action

Layout, the Experience

3.2.2
Perception of
the Layout

Hearing and feeling
the layout

Hearing and feeling the layout

At the point where the traditional media reach their limits is where digital media really become exciting: dynamics, sound, interactivity. But to what extent can the sound, for example, influence the perception process within the layout? Sound and pictures often have a direct connection, since they are already stored in our memory as experiences. The picture of a Caribbean beach with the corresponding music immediately provokes an emotional reaction – just as the wrong music would lead to irritation.

Mood: www.batida.com

The right Caribbean feeling needs the right music. At least it is a wonderful way of strengthening the visual impression of a layout. Music as the trigger for moods is a classical advantage of digital media over print media. This makes it considerably more effective.

Information: Coloreader

The "coloreader" project by the designer Daniel Rothaug translates colours into acoustic triads. RGB colour values are broken down and mathematically transcribed on to one or more octaves. Thus visual information can be made discernible on an acoustic level of perception and enriched by an additional information level.

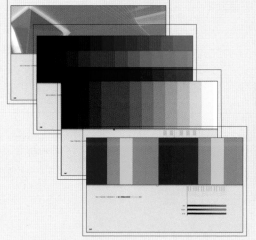

www.audiotourism.com

Original sounds supplement the visual image.

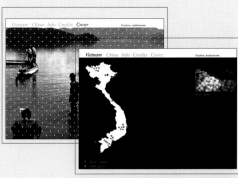

Audible icons

Sounds correspond to a real noise and illustrate the actions on the screen. They reinforce and confirm the experience made by interaction.

Earcons

These sounds are specially designed and serve the audible labelling of actions on the screen. As they have no basis in real life, they add to the experience.

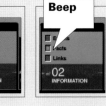

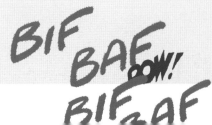

Yet sounds can also complement what we see in the layout, its information content: the explanatory text or original sound of an event lend the image value-added information. And sounds as audible markers can also contribute to a better differentiation in our perception – which is not possible or desirable on the visual level within the layout, for example.

Tactile characteristics within the digital layout are mainly determined by the physical characteristics of the interface. In most cases this is the mechanical resistance of the mouse button, joystick or that of a touch-sensitive surface. We know how a button or slider works, for example, from the real world. A corresponding representation on the screen conveys to us in a second the same function – no less, but also no more.

Simulated characteristics

The most obvious principle for a transfer of the real into the virtual world: three-dimensional appearances are adapted for the display, so as to convey functional characteristics.

Please do touch

The representation of real, physical characteristics, such as three-dimensional elevations or the lines on a surface make it clear that there is something to click on or move.

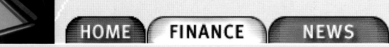

www.gsup.de

"Scratching" over the area with the mouse long enough reveals a picture. A principle that plays with the user's curiosity and transforms the mechanical effect of friction to the display.

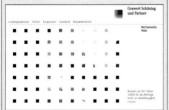
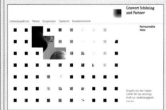

www.yugop.com

The computer mouse becomes a digital paintbrush within the virtual space: a well-known principle really – yet completely different. Real processes are not simply copied: they are expanded by characteristics and effects, which would be impossible in physical reality.

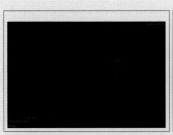

Seeing within the layout

Under normal circumstances our eyes are incredibly powerful – and equally sensitive. Looking at an illuminated display strains the eyes more than a reflective information medium (e.g. paper). Colours and contrasts are perceived more intensively on the display, differences in brightness compared to the surrounding light have to be constantly compensated for and dynamic elements need to be refocused more frequently. We resolve many questions resulting from the layout intuitively during the design process due to our own experience and personal taste.

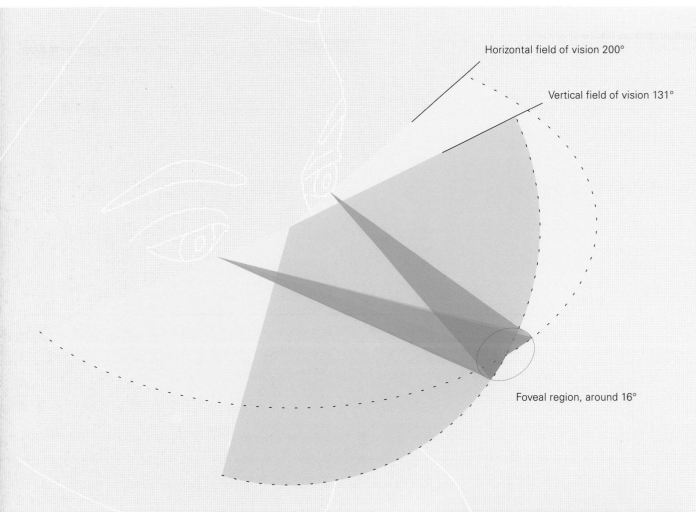

Horizontal field of vision 200°

Vertical field of vision 131°

Foveal region, around 16°

Foveal region

At a distance of ca. 50 cm from the display, the entire layout may be within the field of vision, but only one area (the foveal region) measuring ca. 15 x 2.5 cm may be sharply perceived at a glance. Layout elements larger than this area are scanned line by line from top to bottom. If certain elements are to be perceived quickly then it makes sense to have them correspond to the size of the foveal region.

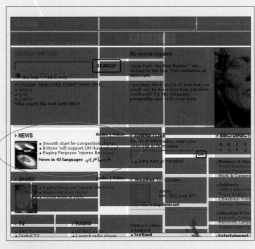

In so doing we tend to quickly overburden the user's actual powers of vision. The guidelines resulting from common studies on user-friendliness are as manifold as the applications investigated. But even a look at the physiological characteristics of the eye can help a lot in answering basic questions.

Marginal contrast intensification

In areas of low contrast, such as black-and-white edges, the eye intensifies these contrasts (marginal contrast intensification), so as to differentiate among the visible objects more easily. We have seen this effect in the "Hermann grid", where grey dots appear although in reality there are none. A similar effect occurs with the visible pixels on the display: at the edges the eye intensifies the contrast, which is why we often notice the staircase-like effect in particular. Only two things can help here: reducing the contrast, as with anti-aliasing; or a correspondingly high resolution, so that smaller pixels lead to fewer contrast edges, and the overall appearance becomes less busy.

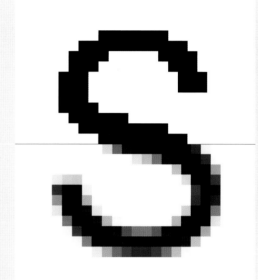

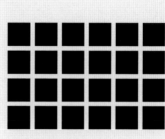

Hermann grid illusion

Resolution of an image

The composition of an image made up of pixels means that we really see two things when we look at a layout: the appearance of the layout and the technical nature of the image. This effect is more or less apparent depending on the distance to and resolution of the display – the ideal representation remains, of course, one without characteristics determined by resolution.

Resolution of the human eye

The eye's resolution is ca. 0.0016 degrees of the field of vision. This means, for example, that we can still see an area of ca. 2 x 2 m at a distance of 10 m – and, likewise, a monitor on our desk needs to have a resolution of ca. 175 dpi before we can no longer see its pixels.

Distance

Resolutions necessary for the technical characteristics (e.g. pixels, grid dots) of an image to become invisible.

Distance	0.25 m	0.5 m	5 m	10 m
Resolution	350 dpi	175 dpi	20 dpi	10 dpi

Perception – typography

Apart from the visual impression made by a font, its application on the display screen in a mode suitable for the media is a central topic in layout design. As such, the aspects of subjective font perception can hardly be separated from those of the technical representation. No matter which font is chosen, its suitability for the chosen medium always needs to be comprehensively tested in a series of experiments.

Font and font size

Sans-serif fonts (here Univers 55) are easier to display and read on the screen in smaller type sizes. The details of a serif font (here Sabon) may mean that the contours lose their sharpness when the type size is too small. Nowadays, fonts can easily be embedded in digital documents or made available on Web servers. Cross-platform standard fonts such as Arial or Geneva are thus no longer the ultimate choice for a uniform layout appearance. Of greater significance is the choice of type size, since this determines the sharp appearance of the bitmap on the display. Thus a font shown in 13 point may be larger than in 12 point, but in certain circumstances the bitmap may be displayed much more irregularly on the rigid pixel matrix of the computer screen. In general, the rule applies: test fonts exactly down to their bitmap. The higher the display resolution, the more easily different fonts may be used > 3.2.3.

Sabon Roman not anti-aliased/anti-aliased	Univers 55 not anti-aliased/anti-aliased	Point
Hedgow Hedgow	Hedgow Hedgow	6
Hedgow Hedgow	Hedgow Hedgow	9
Hedgow Hedgow	Hedgow Hedgow	10
Hedgow Hedgow	Hedgow Hedgow	12
Hedgow Hedgow	Hedgow Hedgow	13
Hedgow Hedgow	Hedgow Hedgow	14
Hedgow Hedgow	Hedgow Hedgow	16
Hedgow Hedgow	Hedgow Hedgow	18
Hedgow Hedgow	Hedgow Hedgow	20

Line spacing

A somewhat larger line spacing is recommended for displaying on the computer screen: ca. 140 per cent of the type size is a good guideline, giving the text a smooth appearance. Much larger line spacing, on the other hand, may lead to the eye missing the start of the next line while reading.

Type size	Capital height		
	8 px.	Hg	
10 px.			Line spacing
		Hg	14 px.

Line length

Line lengths on the display are ideal when they can be perceived by the eye at a glance. This example contains around 45–55 characters per line. Shorter lines may lead to the contents being "torn apart" due to too many leaps of the eye while reading, while longer lines make it difficult to find the start of the following line.

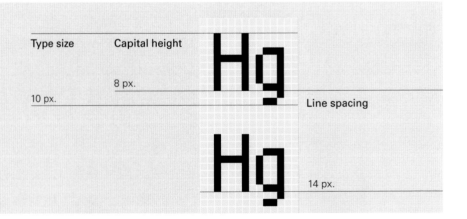

```
    5    10   15   20   25   30   35   40   45   50
Lorem ipsum dolor sit amet, consectetuer adipiscing
sed diam nonummy nibh euismod tincidunt ut laoreet
dolore magna aliquam erat volutpat. Ut wisi enim
ad minim veniam, quis nostrud exerci tation ullamcor
per suscipit lobortis nisl ut aliquip ex ea commodo.
Duis autem vel eum iriure dolor in hendrerit in vulp
utate velit esse molestie consequat, vel illum dolore
    5    10   15   20   25   30   35   40   45   50
```

Different factors decisively influence how text is read on the display screen. Apart from the limitations imposed by the resolution, it is mainly the fact that text nearly always has to compete with considerably more visual impressions than is the case with print media, for example. This has contributed to reading habits on the display screen being adjusted to the reading requirements. Text is now more often selectively glanced over, rather than read linearly. The eye is constantly on the look out for prominent fixation points that allow a fast "scanning" of texts. And wherever longer passages are properly read, the ones that work the best are those where the external influences are reduced to a minimum.

Structuring

Paragraphs make a text clearer and arouse a desire to read. Thus, paragraphs should be inserted wherever it makes sense in terms of the content – and occasional short "reading breaks" also help above and beyond this. Unstructured acres of text, on the other hand, only inhibit reading.

Lorem ipsum? Dolor sit amet, consectetuer adipiscing nonummy nibh euismod tincidunt ut laoreet dolore magna erat volutpat. Ut wisi enim ad minim veniamquis nostrud ullamcorper suscipit lobortis nisl ut aliquip ex ea.

Duis autem vel eum iriure dolor in hendrerit in vulputate molestie consequat, vel illum dolore eu feugiat nulla eros et accumsan et iusto odio dignissim qui blandit pra zzril delenit augue duis dolore te feugait nulla facilisi. dolor sit amet, consectetuer adipiscing elit, sed diam euismod tincidunt ut laoreet dolore magna aliquam erat

Ut wisi enim? Ad minim veniam, quis nostrud exerci suscipit lobortis nisl ut aliquip ex ea commodo consequat. Autem vel eum iriure dolor in hendrerit in vulputat esse.

Capitalisation

Mixed capitalisation gives the individual words a characteristic image, making them more readily distinguishable for the reader. However, using only capitals considerably slows down the flow of reading.

Lorem ipsum dolor sit amet, consectetuer adipiscing sed diam nonummy nibh euismod tincidunt ut laoreet dolore magna aliquam erat volutpat. Ut wisi enim

LOREM IPSUM DOLOR SIT AMET, CONSECTETUER ADIPISCING SED DIAM NONUMMY NIBH EUSIMOD TINCIDUNT UT LAOREET DOLORE MAGNA ALIQUAM ERAT VOLUPTAT. UT WISI ENIM

Justification

Left justified (right ragged) texts are the easiest to read. The raggedness on the right side quickly guides the eye to the following line and to its beginning. Right-justified text results in the opposite effect – the ragged beginnings of the lines are difficult to find. Justified type is further hindered by the word spacing being of varying size: here the flow of reading is even disturbed within the line itself.

Lorem ipsum dolor sit amet, consectetuer adipiscing elit, sed diam nonummy nibh euismod tincidunt ut laoreet dolore magna aliquam erat.

Ut wisi enim ad minim veniam, quis nostrud exerci tation ullamcorper suscipit lobortis nisl ut aliquip ex ea commodo consequat. Duis autem vel eum iriure dolor in hendrerit in vulputate velit esse molestie

Lorem ipsum dolor sit amet, consectetuer adipiscing elit, sed diam nonummy nibh euismod tincidunt ut laoreet dolore magna aliquam erat.

Ut wisi enim ad minim veniam, quis nostrud exerci tation ullamcorper suscipit lobortis nisl ut aliquip ex ea commodo consequat. Duis autem vel eum iriure dolor in hendrerit in vulputate velit esse molestie

Lorem ipsum dolor sit amet, consectetuer adipiscing elit, sed diam nonummy nibh euismod tincidunt ut laoreet dolore magna aliquam erat.

Ut wisi enim minim veniam, quis nostrud exerci tation ullamcorper suscipit lobortis nisl ut aliquip ex ea commodo consequat. Duis autem vel eum iriure dolor in hendrerit in vulputate velit esse molestie

Type contrast

Both negative and positive text are almost equally legible. White text on a dark background appears slightly larger due to the illumination at the edges. Adequate contrast between the text and its background is important, although the maximum contrast, such as black/white, should be avoided. Most readers find a careful reduction of the contrast more pleasant, since the text is perceived as less busy.

Lorem ipsu sed diam n dolore mag

Perception – colour

The perception of colours always triggers emotional reactions. This makes them an extremely powerful conveyer of information within the layout. Emotional reactions can seldom be generalised, if at all. What may be a friendly, fresh light green for one person is an unbearable bilious green for another. Here the personal tastes are only a part of the individual colour perception. Added to this are the aspects of the contextual contents or those of the cultural surroundings. Yet some aspects of colour perception may be reliably incorporated in the layout design, especially to signal colours, recollection and perception of contrasts.

Different perceptions of colours

Colour spectrum
The eye processes light from a wide range of frequencies: from 780 nm (red) to 380 nm (violet).

The retina
The retina contains the receptors responsible for colour perception. However, their sensitivity is not equally distributed over the entire frequency range: 64 per cent are mainly sensitive to red, 32 per cent to green and only 2 per cent to blue.

Different colour sensitivity
This unequal distribution of receptors leads to an unequal colour perception. This is why red has a much greater signal effect than black, white or grey, for example.

www.samsung.com
Not necessarily colourful, yet with great signal effect – red as a visual stimulus.

www.haiku.it
Totally uncolourful, but not without colour – a beautiful, colourful world of black and white.

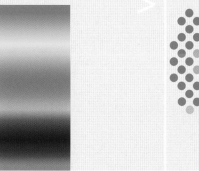
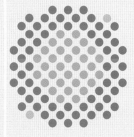

Quantity table

16,000,000	colours are theoretically perceivable by humans
192,000	colour graduations can be distinguished
10,000	colour graduations on the display are indeed perceivable
200	we can give names to around 200 colour graduations
7	we can recall a maximum of seven colours after a few seconds

The fact that colour can be used practically for free in digital media does not necessarily make the layout design any easier. Very often the exact opposite is the case: in the mainly colourful world of digital media, a skilful use of colour is a particular challenge, one best met by considering the fundamental basics of colour perception.

Contrasts

A prerequisite for the differentiated perception of a shape is its "contrasting" appearance. Only then does text become legible or an image recognisable, for example. When thinking of contrasts we automatically turn to the best known, such as complementary or light/dark contrasts. Yet there are more than just these:

Complementary contrast
Complementary colours provide the most strongly perceived contrast effect. This is particularly true of the primary colour pairs yellow-violet, green-red and blue-orange.

Simultaneous contrast
The eye "corrects" colours, so as to ensure a maximum difference from the background. Thus the same colour appears lighter or darker depending on the background.

Quality contrast
Also called an intensity contrast: a pure colour is perceived more intensively if it is surrounded by lightened or darkened graduations.

Quantity contrast
Colours are perceived more or less intensively. Different coloured parts of an area can thus create a strongly contrasting tension.

Light/dark contrast
Darkly coloured areas are perceived more intensively and larger than areas with a light colour. The greater the difference, the larger the signal effect.

Cold/warm contrast
A contrast revealing the different emotional qualities of individual colours, perceived as "cold" or "warm". Cold colours also appear distant, while warm colours seem closer.

Cultural meanings

On the Internet in particular the use of colour repeatedly highlights the phenomenon of different cultural meanings. While red means good luck in China, in Egypt it is the colour of mourning, to name but one striking example. It is worthwhile bearing these different meanings in mind and weighing up when a cultural adaptation of the colour scheme is called for and when not.

Luck	Death/mourning	Strength	Danger	Virtue	Religion
China	Egypt	Japan	USA	Europe	Buddhism
Egypt	India	Arab countries	Europe	USA	Islam
Japan	China	USA	Japan	India	
Germany	Japan	Europe		Arab countries	
Ghana	Europe	Egypt			
Brazil	USA	Malaysia			
Pakistan	Africa				

			Prosperity	Modernity	Safety
			China	Japan	USA
			India	Europe	Europe

Colour: adaptation

Alongside the brand name, the Coca-Cola logo is based above all on the colour red. In Western cultures it dominates the branding (as in Brazil), while in Turkey and China the colour is considerably reduced.

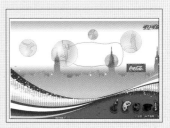

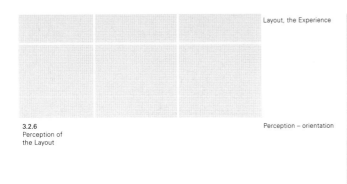

Perception – orientation

The good news first: adapting the power of orientation within a layout is much more manageable than you might suppose – at least where a medium is used where the user has learned to adapt to constantly new requirements. And now the bad news: this willingness to adapt soon reaches its limits if it does not quickly lead to success. This is then a very brief summary of what we can learn from numerous usability studies.

Mental models

The key questions in orientation are: Where am I? How can I get to where I want to go? How do I get back to my starting point? What are my options? A mental model of the surroundings forms the basis for answering such queries. The layout can help the user develop as exact a mental model as possible.

www.allegra.de

The storeys metaphor appeals to a familiar orientation pattern and thus facilitates comprehension of the structure.

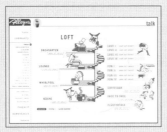

www.mvrdv.nl

The thematic structure here is the subject of the home page – even abstract visualisations of the system structure allow a suitable mental model to be formed.

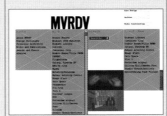

The right balance

Decisive for the correct structuring of a digital application is an optimal adaptation of the structure to the contents provided. A strict orientation along schematic structures unfortunately often leads to few ordered results. The proven 7 (+/– 2) scheme can thus only be an aid in promoting the clarity and recognisability of structured contents.

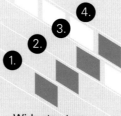

Deep structure

Provides on one level just a few options and is thus easier to comprehend. But it requires more choices of direction on the part of the user, and more levels and steps are necessary in order to reach the actual destination.

Wide structure

Offers more choices and leads to the desired information via fewer levels and in fewer steps. But if the options are not clearly named or badly structured then the structure soon becomes puzzling.

In terms of layout design this means that a concurring adaptation of layout structures to conventional patterns is not absolutely necessary, even if the user can quickly comprehend a "surprising", innovative structure. In theory this sounds simple, but in practice? It is decisive to know here that every user develops in his/her cognitive process a "mental model" of their surroundings – for example, of a visited website. These models allow the user to orientate themselves among the contents, structure and functions of a digital application. The more the user's mental model corresponds to the real structure, the faster and more effectively he/she will be able to orientate themselves.

This may be achieved by using metaphors: the desktop, as used in various computer operating systems, is no doubt the best-known example. Yet if the connections to reality are too close they may prove to be restrictive and obscure the view of that which is innovative and pioneering, because in the formation of a fitting mental model it is important to make the existing structures transparent – and this can quite easily be accomplished in a completely abstract manner.

Eye movement

Most studies of eye movement while visiting websites reveal that it is schematic. Firstly, the focus is on the middle, then on the left and finally on the top right corner. At least this can generally be said about unfamiliar sites. If, however, the characteristics of the layout are already known from previous visits, the familiar areas within the layout are directly focused upon.

Preferences

Text or image? The age-old competition seems to be settled where current information is concerned: on news and portal sites with many components headlines are clearly preferred to images.

Relevance

There are distinct, hierarchic expectations made of the ordering process within the contents.
The most important and the most current contents are found at the top. And vice versa: it is assumed that contents further down are of less relevance – especially when they are outside the visible window.

Accents

When it comes to perceiving digital information we tend to use the term "scanning" rather than reading. Thus it is important that a digital layout sets sufficient accents, such as typographic or graphic highlights, and thus allows a quick overview of the information.

Accessibility

Accessibility in relation to digital media means that these are especially prepared while bearing in mind the needs of disabled users. This topic extends as far as the spectrum of physical, mental and sensual restrictions. Yet with regard to layout design there are some central aspects that should be discussed in connection with human perception. Technical aspects, which are mainly concerned with programming and media specifications, are excluded here, but further resources are given in the appendix. Accessibility is both a necessity and a chance. It is not so much a restriction to the freedom of design, but rather an extension of it. It presents the opportunity to recheck one's design in terms of its fundamental logical consistency and

Colour choice
Colour blindness occurs much more often than one would expect, especially red-green blindness. This is where yellow-green and red-orange values are difficult to distinguish. Colours need to have high contrasts to remain distinguishable. This can be easily tested by viewing the layout in greyscales.

Text formats
Screen-readers convert the written text into spoken words – this is often the only chance for people with impaired vision to use digital media. However, this presupposes that the text is integrated in the layout in a readable format (e.g. ASCII). Thus, in this example, not only the information texts but also the navigation is included in a "readable" format.

Freedom from the mouse
Predetermined tabulators, for users whose mobility is so restricted that they cannot navigate using the mouse, can facilitate the function of a page. This then allows navigation through the layout solely using the keyboard. In addition, the currently selected link is visually highlighted.

comprehensibility – a prerequisite demanded not only by disabled people but also by most regular users. There are basically two ways of preparing suitable layouts: the specifications are adhered to within the layout, or a parallel system is developed, offering a greatly reduced, text-only version. This may well be easier to realise, but is often rightly criticised as being an excluding form of disabled access.

Accessibility refers to all layout components important for using the interface, such as navigational, functional, orientation and structural elements. And of course to all other elements needed for an understanding of the information on offer. Conversely, specially made accessible decorative elements or gimmicks do not really contribute to useful accessibility.

It is always problematic when accessibility is to be integrated at a later date once the interface has been completed. Seen technically, with early planning, any layout can be made for disabled access. Thus it is important to incorporate in the conception and planning the features in question from the start. Furthermore, it is naturally useful to know about the technical functions that allow accessibility by way of user-controlled systems, such as browsers, the operating system's help functions or helpful input and output devices.

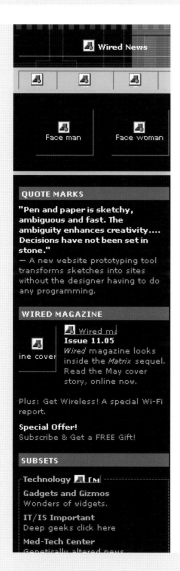

Readable images

Images are difficult to translate into words, meaning that complex visual information is often hidden from users with screen-readers. A description of the images can at least partly compensate for this, using alternate tags in the HTML code that can be read by the screen-reader, for example. This is particularly important where the navigation is by way of images.

Equivalent contents

Another possibility for representing visual information for disabled people is so-called "titles". These allow images and links to be supplemented by additional comments or descriptions. This represents an additional level of information for all users – one which can also be read by the screen-reader.

Text size

Text on the screen is often too small – not just for users with impaired vision. To be able to change the font size the text must be editable. Once this is ensured, the text size can be set in the browser – often affecting the layout, however. As an alternative, the layout concept may consider different font sizes, which may be integrated as functions of the interface, thus maintaining control of the appearance. Even "real" zoom functions, as with web browsers, enlarge the image displayed and aid better legibility.

3.3.0

One layout – many faces

Probably the only time a digital layout shows its "true face" is just before it is put to use. Once it is "online" or "rolled out" the operating technical requirements can greatly deviate from the original development environment – especially the user's visual preferences. A user has numerous opportunities to use his/her own settings to influence the representation of the layout. In the worst case, the layout is hardly recognisable when in use.

The original: www.wz-berlin.de
With normal monitor use and unchanged standard browser settings the page is represented as the designer intended.

Colour set-up of the monitor
The hardware alone can greatly influence the layout.

System set-up: accessibility options
All Windows systems allow for a more "reader-friendly" set-up. In this example "Contrast" was selected.

The design of a digital layout is a balancing act between many variables. Hardware, software and the user-specific settings – it almost seems as though the design of digital media is a constant design of compromises.

What may be sensible on the user side in terms of technical aspects is highly debatable when the communicative side is taken into consideration. If, for example, we consider the communicative aims in the choice of colours, specific aspects of perception or even strict rules for a consistent image as part of the corporate design, it soon becomes apparent why questions of design sometimes have to be solved without compromise.

Even the constant adaptation of a design to the scope and pace of technical developments may quickly become a Sisyphean task: the primary alignment towards these factors seldom allows the development of a constant and consistent design solution. Here, decisions are called for that result in secure planning for a certain period of application use – so that with the next relaunch the technical and design modifications can be equally consistently implemented.

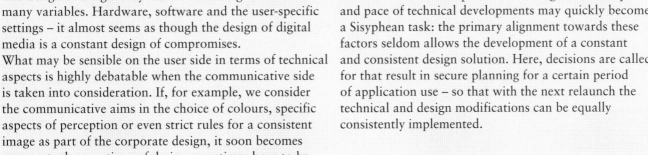

About the WZB

Basic social science resea
the general theme of „devel
democratic societies." The
the cross-national compara

The WZB is well integrated
linked to scientific activity in
research contributes to both
in the social sciences. In ac
this mostly empirical work i
political scientists, econom
the WZB. The western indu
interest. Research on centr
transformation processes,
Europeanization and globa

Intense cooperation has de
Britain, France, the Netherla

Sebstverständnis des WZ

WZB About

Basic social science research is c
„ developmental trends, problem
solving capacities of social and g
from approaches taken in other

The WZB is well integrated int
scientific activity in the universi
the treatment of practical issues
international comparative perspe
for sociologists, political scientist
WZB. The western industrialize
central and eastern European co
1990s. Increasing attention is nov

Intense cooperation has develope

WZB About

Basic social science re
society under the gene
innovation in modern de
governmental institutio
to learn from approach

The WZB is well integra
scientific activity in th
the treatment of pract
international comparat
for sociologists, politic
the WZB. The western
on central and eastern
the 1990s. Increasing
well.

Browser option: no images
No photos are shown, but also no elements integrated as images, such as the logo. Parts of the navigation are also no longer visible.

Browser option: own fonts
With this setting a serif font was selected instead of the default sans-serif Arial/Geneva. This alters the line breaks and greatly hinders the legibility.

Browser option: no style sheets
Style sheets are the central instrument for fixing the characteristics of a layout. If they are blocked, then there are serious changes to the layout.

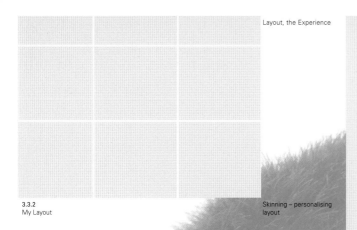

Skinning – personalising
layout

Skinning – personalising layout

A whole separate group of digital applications is characterised by the possibility of altering a layout according to personal preferences. They allow an "explicit personalisation": users can access the layout to a pre-defined extent. The aim is to bond users more strongly to "their" layout and so underscore the service idea behind an application. This is achieved, for example, with the selection of image motifs, colours or fonts. What is surprising is that just a few, targeted changes to the layout can result in a completely different image.

1. Choice of colour scheme
A preference-setting page allows the choice of variable parameters. As a first step, the colour scheme is altered using pre-defined combinations.

2. Layout arrangement
A change to the layout structure: from three to two columns. The contents inside the columns can also be moved.

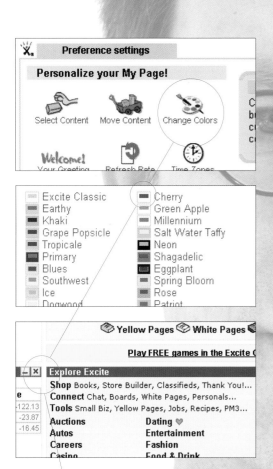

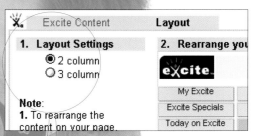

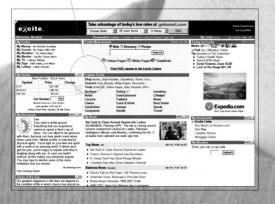

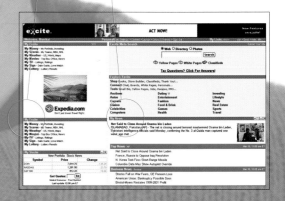

A layout where it is not known how it might look later presupposes a great number of systematic design features: all components need to be designed in a highly modular fashion. The ordering system needs to contain simple structures and allow a combination of modules, such as in columns. Permanent elements require areas within the layout, which are exempt from the sphere of influence and signal this by way of their exposed position.

3. Background motif

Background motifs can be selected from a list of topics. Then the colour scheme is adapted to the personal preferences.

4. Change of text size and colour

Here the text size is increased and the colour adapted – and the personalised layout is finished. As a result, the larger text has shifted the entire page layout.

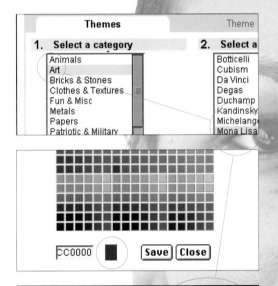

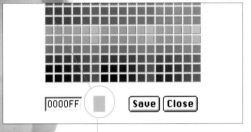

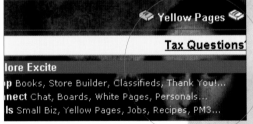

Personalising contents

Interactive media may be described as interest media. The term "interest media" here means specifically that users can practically decide for themselves how, when and why they concern themselves with these media. This does not only apply to the choice between different websites, but also to the individual selection of information and its adaptation to their personal interests within one and the same website.

Personalising contents

1. Compiled headlines

Depending on the amount of information required, the type and number of topics in the "Headline" area can be adjusted, as well as the number of reports on each topic.

2. Local weather

The default here – not surprisingly – is the weather report for Washington, DC. However, the forecast can be set to the user's home town. In this example, New York has been selected.

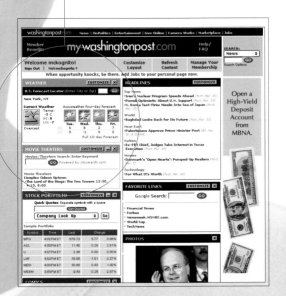

The possibilities for an "explicit personalisation" of information are aimed – as opposed to changes to the image – less at "beautifying" the layout, but much more at optimising the information: to create an overview of the endless amount on offer on the Internet and so see at a glance what is important and interesting.
The personalisation of information works within a pre-defined spectrum of possible choices. And it, too, presupposes a clear structuring of the layout: simple divisions into columns and units, unmistakable definition of the size of the graphical elements and a consistent labelling of all the components.

Yet as opposed to alterations to the layout >3.3.2, users expect from a personalisation of the contents that the layout will be shown in its usual manner and be equally consistently coded – i.e. as few surprises as possible, such that orientation and function are still perfectly guaranteed. In almost every case, the personalisation of the contents results in a change to the layout, even if this is usually only noticeable upon closer inspection.

3. Cinema programme

The extent of the individual news units may be altered. Here there is much interest in the cinema programme – consequently the scope of the programme shown has been extended to include other cinemas.

4. Removal of a rubric

Undesired rubrics may be removed with a single mouse click – and the individual news page is finished.

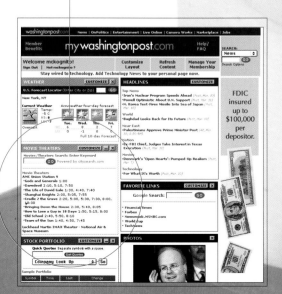

3.3.4
My Layout

Implicit individualisations –
the software helps

Implicit individualisations – the software helps

Interaction with digital media also allows changes to the contents and layout that the user did not necessarily consciously initiate, and yet results in a personal adaptation. Individualisations, which are mostly carried out by the medium itself, may be termed "implicit". They are divided into three groups. Firstly, those that filter user groups according to defined rules and then trigger certain adaptations (rule-based filtering). Secondly, individualisations that filter the users' interests according to classified contents and thus allow a corresponding optimisation of the contents (content-based filtering).

Rule-based filtering

Simple, strictly standardised rules initiate an individual adaptation of the contents and layout: The user's origins (taken from the browser language version) lead to corresponding languages, contents and a suitable layout. Registration at a website identifies the user and thus the content on offer can be optimised, for example, by providing new, unvisited pages.

Content-based filtering

All contents correspond to clear categories and are uniformly classified. The user's interests are met with correspondingly similar contents. This requires very dynamic and flexible structures within the layout, as it can never be predicted how many hits really correspond to the interests.

www.ge.com
The visitor's language is determined by querying the language version of the browser – sending the user straight away to the relevant language pages on the site

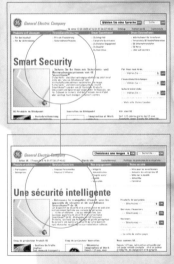

www.mini.com
Return visits to the site lead to the visitor being met with a friendly, personalised layout.

www.warehouse.com
A strict categorisation of the products allows links to related articles.

And finally individualisations that compare the interests and behaviour of individual users with others and thus are able to make suitable offers based on behavioural and interest patterns (collaborative filtering).

The aim of each system-controlled individualisation is to make the best possible match between what the digital application has to offer and the users' interests. This naturally also affects the layout: from the preparation of different layout variations, the integration of individualised modules right up to the graphical labelling of individually arranged components. Whenever the system initiates an automated process as part of the individualisation, this process has to be visually understandable for the user.

At the same time, the alterations need to be so differentiated so as not to create the impression of offering the user something completely new. The basic requirement for such applications is a modular structure, together with a clear concept for the possible graphical coding by way of colours, typographic highlights or labelled image elements. Design work on a system that can be personalised is a matter of working on fine details – and requires the creation of a visual leeway for flexible adaptations so as to allow for an unmistakable image.

Collaborative filtering

The exact tracking of user interests provides a clear profile of the user – without the need for registration. As opposed to other filtering methods, the user profile here is not compared to rules or classified offers, but with the profiles of other users. Matches are firstly sought among the users' interests, so as to make even more personalised offers. This type of individualisation provides a wide range of customised results and thus presupposes the highest degree of flexibility within the layout, too.

www.amazon.com

The classic example of implicit individualisation: All the filter types are combined to produce an optimised individual offer. Only the frame is defined by the Amazon layout. The results are kept as neutral as possible, but consistently coded, such as colour coding of the typography.

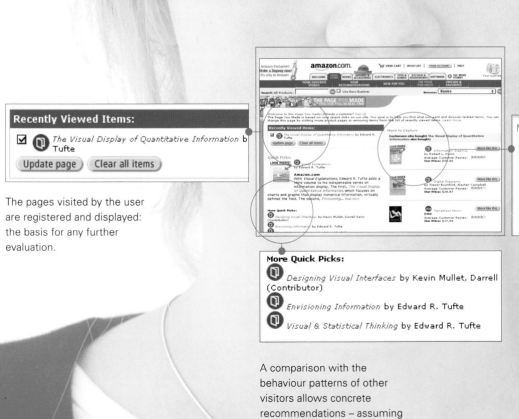

Recently Viewed Items:

☑ 📖 *The Visual Display of Quantitative Information* by Tufte

(Update page) (Clear all items)

The pages visited by the user are registered and displayed: the basis for any further evaluation.

More Quick Picks:

📖 *Designing Visual Interfaces* by Kevin Mullet, Darrell (Contributor)

📖 *Envisioning Information* by Edward R. Tufte

📖 *Visual & Statistical Thinking* by Edward R. Tufte

A comparison with the behaviour patterns of other visitors allows concrete recommendations – assuming similar interests among entire groups.

More to Explore

Customers who bought The Visual Display of Quantita Information **also bought:**

LOOK INSIDE
Information Graphics

📖 Information Graphics
by Robert L. Harris
Average Customer Review: ★★
Our Price: $50.00

Relatively close: recommended books closely related by subject, based on a consistent, thematic classification of the products.

No more layout?

No more layout?

In the world of digital media the layout's area of application also has its limits. The distribution of data and information in digital media is not actually necessarily bound to a visually designed form, such as a website. In strict terms, it is even one of the fundamental ideas of the Internet to make information available that may be used in repeatedly new contexts and combinations. The separation of form and content, such as with some XML-based data formats, leads to a dissolving of the traditional meaning of layout, whereby the unit of content and form is meant to be understood as an integrated product.
If these are now separated, content and form could each

Whose layout?

The Web provider Crayon allows the compilation of an individual news site, made up of parts of other websites. The default frame is deliberately unassuming.

News aggregators

The RSS data format allows the integration of standardised news text across the most varied range of platforms. Here, the layout always originates with the software used – not with the original from the data provider.

The original:
www.nasa.gov/news

Original source:
www.wired.com

Integrated in
www.crayon.net

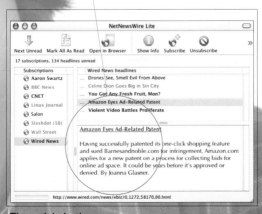

The article in the news aggregator
NetNewsWire

stem from two different sources, which might not know about each other and so cannot align their offers with one another. Examples of this are websites that compile their information from other websites or software programs (news aggregators) that make their information available using special file formats (e.g. RSS/RDF) and only use the Internet as a transport route.

It is almost impossible for layouts without pre-defined contents to link up with these and connotatively support their dissemination. They are forced to remain neutral and mainly take on tasks in data organisation, user-navigation and distribution. Thus, a separation of content and form leads to a completely individual type of communication, where the form is no longer a direct part of the message.

The automated distribution of documents becomes the main distribution of information, which needs to be strictly standardised specifically for this purpose. This neutralised information may be easily disseminated, yet it has no autonomous image. Conversely, the very layouts of such standardised systems may often be personalised in the ways described above. The consequence of this is something that no longer has anything to do with the actual synthesis of form and content.

Thus here we need to find new forms of expression – one of the major challenges for work on the new layout.

Translation robots

Separation of the content from the form – and the return of the content into a new form. What role does the layout play, if it is ignored following the translation? What is the value of the information provided by the translation without the layout?

PDF > HTML

The original and its copy – here the content and form were originally separated so as to be ultimately joined together again according to apparently formal criteria. Automated document generators are intended to simplify working with digitally distributed information.

No layout please!

In many cases a complex layout is quite simply undesirable. Users usually prefer a text-only version for technical reasons (loading times, print output, etc.).

www.wired.com

Title page of a PDF
(www.commerzbank.de/aktionaere)

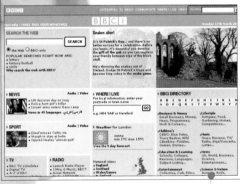

www.bbc.com

Translated by
www.google.de

HTML version of the PDF by
www.google.de

Text version

Bibliography

Against Method
Paul Feyerabend
W W Norton & Co, 1993

Bildkonzepte
Peter Jenny
Verlag Hermann Schmidt
Mainz, 2000

Ein Bild ist mehr als ein Bild
Christian Doelker
Klett-Cotta, 1997

Business Knowledge
Management
Volker Bach, Petra Vogler,
Hubert Österle
Springer Verlag, 1999

Compendium for Literates
Karl Gerstner
The MIT Press, 1975

Computers as Theatre
Brenda Laurel
Addison Wesley, 1991

2D Visual Perception
Moritz Zwimpfer
Verlag Niggli AG, 1994

Design By Numbers
John Maeda
The MIT Press, 1999

Design Writing Research
Ellen Lupton, J. Abbott Miller
Princeton Architectural
Press, 1995

The Designer and the Grid
Lucienne Roberts, Julia Thrift
RotoVision SA, 2002

Designing visual interfaces
Kevin Mullet, Darrell Sano
SunSoft Press, 1995

Experience Design
Nathan Shedroff
New Riders, 2001

Farbhunger
Peter Jenny
Verlag Hermann Schmidt
Mainz, 2000

Handbuch der
Kommunikationsguerilla
L. Blissett, S. Brünzels
Verlag Libertäre Assoziation,
2001

The Humane Interface
Jef Raskin
Addison-Wesley, 2001

Interface
Gui Bonsiepe
Bollmann, 1996

Interface Culture
Steven Johnson
Basic Books, 1997

Kleine Medienchronik
Hans H. Hiebel
Beck'sche Reihe, 1997

The Language of New Media
Lev Manovich
The MIT Press, 2001

Lesetypographie
Hans Peter Willberg,
Friedrich Forssmann
Verlag Hermann Schmidt
Mainz, 1997

Macintosh Human Interface
Guidelines
Apple Computer Inc.
Addison-Wesley, 1992

Maeda@Media
John Maeda
Universe Books, 2001

Map in Minds
Roger M. Downs, David Stea
HarperCollins, 1977

Mapping
Roger Fawcett-Tang
RotoVision, 2002

Mapping Cyberspace
Martin Dodge, Rob Kitchin
Routledge, 2001

Mapping Websites
Paul Kahn, Kris Lenk
RotoVision, 1995

The Measurement of Meaning
Osgood/Suci/Tannenbaum
University of Illinois Pr
(Pro Ref), 1967

Montage und Collage
Hanno Möbius
Wilhelm Fink Verlag, 2000

Navigation for the Internet and
other Digital Media
Studio 7.5
AVA Publishing SA, 2002

Raster Systeme
Josef Müller-Brockmann
Niggli, 1988

Remediation
Jay David Bolter, Richard Grusin
The MIT Press, 2000

Tacho 3 – Medien, Kunst,
Kommunikation
Karlsruhe, 1992

Vom Tafelbild zum globalen
Datenraum
Peter Weibel
Zentrum für Kunst und Medien-
technologie Karlsruhe, 2001

Understanding Media
Marshall McLuhan
Gingko Press, 2003

Vom Wort zum Bild
Werner Gaede
Wirtschaftsverlag
Langen-Müller/Herbig, 1992

Warum die Liebe rot ist
Rudolf Gross
Econ, 1981

Wie Farben wirken
Eva Heller
Rowohlt, 1991

The Windows Interface
Guidelines for Software Design
Microsoft Corporation
Microsoft Press, 1995

Zeichen über Zeichen
Dieter Mersch
10 Design-Theorie, 1998

Zeichensysteme
Otl Aicher, Martin Krampen
Ernst & Sohn, 1996

Sources and bibliography

0.1-1
Interface
Gui Bonsiepe
Bollmann, 1996

1.1-1
Vom Wort zum Bild
Werner Gaede
Wirtschaftsverlag
Langen-Müller/Herbig, 1992

1.2-1
Lesetypographie
Hans Peter Willberg,
Friedrich Forssmann
Verlag Hermann Schmidt Mainz,
1997

1.3-1
Montage und Collage
Hanno Möbius
Wilhelm Fink Verlag, 2000

1.3-2
The Measurement of
Meaning
Osgood/Suci/Tannenbaum
University of Illinois Pr
(Pro Ref), 1967

Further sources on the Internet

Perception

George A. Miller: The Magical
Number Seven, Plus or Minus
Two: Some limits on our capa-
city for processing information.
Psychological Review, 1956
www.well.com/user/smalin/
miller.html

Robert S. Tannen: Breaking
the Sound Barrier: Designing
Auditory Displays for Global
Usability/en
www.research.att.com/conf/
hfweb/proceedings/tannen/

Aaron Marcus, Edward
Guttman: Globalization of
User-Interface Design for the
Web, 1999
www.amanda.com

Usability

http://psychology.wichita.edu
www.poynterextra.org/et/i.htm
http://zing.ncsl.nist.gov/
www.research.microsoft.com

Accessibility

www.w3.org/WAI/

Links to Internet sites

Chapter 1.2

www.terra.com
www.time.com
www.newscientist.com
www.globalist.com
www.commerzbank.com
www.commerzbanking.de
www.ntt.co.jp
www.lemonde.fr
www.macnews.de
www.harpers.org
www.google.com
www.aldaily.com
www.selfhtml.org
www.c64.com
www.k10k.net
www.nylon.media.mit.edu
www.sodaplay.com
www.asstech.com
www.irrationalcontraption.net
www.hfg-gmuend.de
www.unipublic.unizh.ch
www.ic-berlin.de
www.onemedia.com
www.wz-berlin.de
www.sfmoma.com
www.guggenheim.com
www.izumi.co.jp
www.bankofscotland.co.uk
www.bankgesellschaft.de
www.tibank.bg
www.colmencapital.com
www.jpmorgan.com
www.allianz.com
www.bcl.lu
www.chase.com
www.closept.com
www.ml.com
www.munichre.com
www.taylor-companies.com
www.barbie.com
www.inxight.com
www.craigarmstrong.com
www.kognito.de
www.richardrogers.co.uk
persona.www.media.mit.edu/judith/VisualWho
www.barkowleibinger.com
www.overage4design.com
www.zavesmith.com
www.kostasmurkudis.de
www.isseymiyake.com
www.integral.ruedi-baur.com
www.artemide.com
www.topshop.co.uk
www.huskycz.cz
www.mpib-berlin.mpg.com
www.saab.com
www.dccard.co.jp
www.cmart.design.ru
www.bulthaup.com

Chapter 2.1

www.rempe.de
www.nl-design.net/browserday
www.twoto.com
www.isseymiyake.com
www.ikepod.com
www.triquart-partner.de
www.madxs.com
www.heinlewischerpartner.de
www.helmutlang.com
www.sun.com
www.cnn.com
www.commerzbank.com

Chapter 2.2

www.hp.com
www.nytimes.com
www.albahhar.com
www.oebb.at
www.politie.nl
www.northface.com
www.leica.com
www.bang-olufsen.com
www.transmediale.de
www.sfmoma.com
www.freitag.ch
www.siemens.com
www.siemens-mobile.com
www.fujitsu-siemens.com
www.infineon.com
www.siemens-tts.ch
www.mechoptronics.com
www.vdo.com
www.vdodayton.de
www.my-siemens.com
www.ad.siemens.com
www.siemens.com.eg
www.siemens-mobile.de

Chapter 2.3

www.hvbgroup.com

Chapter 3.1

www.ubs.com
mail.yahoo.com
www.nationalgeographic.com
www.cyberport.de
www.disney.com

Chapter 3.2

www.amazon.com
www.apple.com
www.guardian.co.uk
www.batida.com
www.audiotourism.co.uk
www.freefarm.co.uk
www.gsup.de
www.yugop.com
www.bbc.co.uk
www.samsung.com
www.haiku.it
www.coca-cola.com.tr
www.coca-cola.com.cn
www.cocacolabrasil.com.br
www.allegra.de
www.mvrdv.nl
www.zeit.de
www.washington-post.com
www.dradio.de
www.cnn.com
www.wired.com

Chapter 3.3

www.wz-berlin.de
www.excite.com
www.washington-post.com
www.ge.com
www.mini.com
www.warehouse.com
www.amazon.com
www.nasa.gov/news
www.crayon.net
www.wired.com
www.google.de
www.bbc.com

Further examples

Daniel Rothaug "Coloreader", Sascha Kempe
"Hyperfiction", Erik Adigard, Studio Neue
Gestaltung (Eva Wendel, Daniela Burger,
Hermann Hülsenberg, Pit Stenkhoff) "BRAIN".

Picture credits

Page 118, Coolmuseum, www.coolmuseum.de
Page 125, NASA, www.spaceflight.nasa.gov
All other photographs: kognito, Berlin

Thanks to all the people who lent us their
"...many faces" in chapter 3.3.0.

Thanks to:

Nanette Amann for her daily support –
and patience.

Michael Heimann, Markus Christian
and Nigel J. Luhman for their professional
commitment.

Carola Zwick for her expert management, Brian
Morris for his confidence in this project and
the editorial team at AVA Publishing SA for all
its hard work.

Dörte Beilfuss, Jin-Young Choi, Bernd Göbel,
Marta Pasiek and everybody else at kognito
for their huge support.

**Thanks are also due to the following people
for their help and invaluable contributions to
this book:**

Gui Bonsiepe, Hanno Ehses, Philipp Heidkamp,
Michael Klar, María González de Cosío,
Erich Schöls, Pit Stenkhoff and Oliver Wrede.

Index